# HOW TO WIN AT REAL ESTATE TO BREAK THE FREEDOM BARRIER

# HOW TO WIN AT REAL ESTATE TO BREAK THE FREEDOM BARRIER

*Written and Published By:*
## *Joey Ragona*

*Edited By:*
*Lindsay R. Allison*

# HOW TO WIN AT REAL ESTATE TO BREAK THE FREEDOM BARRIER

Published by Joey Ragona
Copyright 2016 Joey Ragona

ISBN 9780995064003

Printed in Canada

# Contents

# Acknowledgements

The original edition of this book was written, edited and published within a couple of weeks.

But it took over 30 years of trial and error, shifts in mindset, adversity, dedicated people, customers, colleagues and "regular", decent people who just want a better life to provide the inspiration for me to write.

I'm so grateful for my life...and yes, like yours, it's a journey.

In the years since 2005, I have transformed my life through help, support, dedication, and friendships of SO many people.

If it wasn't for my incredible wife Donna, there is no way I would be the man I am today. This book would not have seen the light of day. She is my best friend...my true support and belief with an unconditional love for me. I am truly a fortunate man. She blessed my life with two amazing kids, Matthew and Nicole. I am reminded how amazing the gift of "freedom" and life really is every day. I'm blessed to open my eyes and be with them celebrating even the smallest "wins". Huge hugs and high-fives guys!!

I owe a lot to my parents, especially my dad, for teaching me about business — he was the risk taker, the dreamer, with the "never say it can't be done" attitude — and my mom, the conservative one who always saved for a rainy day. There were a LOT of rainy days.

They both had major impact on how I live and run my own businesses today — I miss you dearly, dad.

Greg Habstritt and Kourosh Assef, my first "real coaches" are people I will forever be indebted to. They introduced me to a new world of possibility, and their caring, understanding, and no B.S. approach to calling me out simply made me a better man.

To my first VIP Mastermind members: Tahani Aburaneh, Jim Sheils, Brian Scrone, Allan Sheiman, Pierre-Paul Turgeon, Ramin Tabibzadeh, Veronica Butler, Brenda Bastell, Wade Fenner, Wade Graham, Dave Peniuk, Joel Hofman, Kim Chernow, John McCabe, Wendy McClelland, Eric Grant — how can I forget you? I remember walking into that room thinking I wasn't good enough to be there…talk about a *Saboteur* mindset. Without your support and encouragement…I don't know where I would be today — thank you.

My other mentors, coaches, trainers: John Assaraf, Eben Pagan, Mike Koenigs, Brendon Burchard, Frank Kern, Ryan Deiss, Joe Polish, Dean Jackson, Jeff Walker, Mel Abraham, Rich Schefren who have helped me improve my business so I can pay it forward to help others.

My friends — the small, but tight-knit group that keep me laughing…

The REIN family: especially Don R. Campbell, Russell Westcott, and Patrick Francey. All of my fellow REIN members and to the ones who have become close friends, supporters, teachers and inspirations in my life — Todor Yordanov, Brian Persaud, Mark Loeffler, Ian Szabo, Quentin D'Souza, Diane Leahy, Aneta Zimnicki, Naushy Saeed…

My real estate teams: Shannon Murree, Diane DiGiandomenico, Rob Hilton, George and Robin Dube, Peter Cuttini, Shayle Rothman, and Garth Chapman.

To ALL my clients, students, and readers...past and present. There are too many of you to list here, but you know who you are. I thank you for your trust in me and my work...because of you, I do what I love every day and it's an honour to serve and support you. I especially want to give a huge SHOUT-OUT to the first person who trusted me and my new coaching career, Trudi Johnson...

I totally want to thank my awesome new friend and Editor Lindsay R. Allison, and her husband-to-be Geoff Edie for putting up with my crazy schedule and providing the sound board to get this project finished in record time.

One last important person I feel compelled to mention: Robert Bonanni — who, as I was writing this book, suddenly passed. I would not feel right if I didn't mention him, not only because he was my best friend, but his death lit another fire under me to get this message out into the world. Because it made me further realize how precious life is, and that we never know how much time we have left. I find so many people with stories and dreams inside of them just WAITING for the right time. WHEN is that right time? RIP brother... I'll miss your sarcastic humour, and the laughs together.

To everyone else: I love supporting you and your dreams. You are all my big "why" and purpose.

—Joey Ragona
Oakville, Ontario

*For Donna, Matthew and Nicole*

# MONIKA AND VAUGHAN JAZYK

I often say, I never knew more about parenting before I had any kids. Today surrounded by 4 wild children, I proudly proclaim that I know nothing. The same goes with real estate investing.

The first night we met Joey at his complimentary group coaching session, we were not there to discover what we did not know, but instead to proudly proclaim what we did know! At least, that was our intention, until Joey put me on the hot seat and we left the coaching session realizing that we.... knew.... NOTHING!

Naked. Vulnerable. Exposed.

These are a few suitable adjectives used to describe my feelings over the following 24 hours. I guess that is how one feels when they are stripped of their notions that they are living the dream as a full time parent AND real estate investor. That their so called "insane busy schedule" that no one in the world but supersonic me could handle is not so busy after all, but instead a sequence of unproductive tasks mustered together to create the illusion of busyness.

And lastly, stripped of my unwavering proclamation that I shouted from the rooftops for the past 5 years....my passion is REAL ESTATE.

Fortunately, my reaction to this revelation **was not to retreat** and continue with these old beliefs, **but to reach out** to Joey and ask for help. He graciously accepted and our coaching journey began. Or so we thought...

Our first meeting was alone with Joey to discuss our 12 month goals. We focused on systemizing our business, creating multiple streams of income, and amplifying our portfolio.

Wait...not so fast!

Although Joey was supportive and respectful of these topical goals, he gently identified some underlying issues that needed to be cleaned up first.

3 years of un-filed taxes and incomplete bookkeeping for 3 corporations (yes, that is 9 returns)!

Cash-sucking properties that would not sell, draining all of our hard-earned income.

Over $250K of debt accumulated from a project that had gone wrong.

Unfortunately, all the supersonic systems in the world could not make these problems go away. These issues needed to be addressed.

But wait! There's more. Some more lessons learned...

Having your kids home and ignoring them for work is NOT spending quality time with your kids.

Going out to work events with your spouse is NOT the same as a date night.

Neglecting your personal growth and enjoyment is NOT necessary to become successful. **Stop putting yourself last!**

So the transformation began, and here we are, about 18 months later....

NO negative cash-flowing properties in our portfolio.

Taxes up to date and filed with yours truly acting as bookkeeper (probably Joey's biggest client accomplishment to date as I HATE accounting).

NO consumer debt!

Revamped schedule in which 80% of my time is devoted to being a wife and a mother, 20% to our business even though....

We are bringing in 4 times income through prioritization and hard work.

And, WE ARE JUST STARTING WITH THE SYSTEMS THAT WILL INCREASE OUR INCOME 5 TIMES MORE PER YEAR!!!

But most importantly, we made a new friend. Joey, we would continue our relationship with you even if you weren't our coach.

We love you. Thank you.

— *Monika and Vaughan Jazyk*

### About Monika and Vaughan

Monika and Vaughan Jazyk chose real estate as an investment vehicle to build passive income and long term wealth for their growing family. After a tumultuous two years of actively investing in a wide range of real estate investment strategies, Monika and Vaughan identified specific real estate models they used to create a successful real estate portfolio and a lifestyle of freedom for themselves and their four young children.

They are the owners of Real Property Investments, a Real Estate Investment Corporation that helps Real People build Real wealth through Real Estate!

As real estate investment specialists and wealth builders, they share these successful models (and their experiences) with others investors, minimizing the investor's risk and maximizing their returns!

**For more information on Real Property Investments visit:**
http://www.rpinvestments.ca/
https://www.facebook.com/mv.jazyk

**Monthly networking group:**
http://www.meetup.com/GTA-Real-Estate-JV-Investors-Networking-Group/

# GARY HIBBERT

There are mental blocks you will have to overcome when you decide to work with a coach. Now these mental blocks can come in different forms, shapes, and sizes for different people. The two most common forms of mental blocks I've seen are:

1. COST. The cost of hiring a coach, and does it make sense financially to do this?

2. EFFECTIVENESS. Will my coach/mentor really be able to help me through my challenges and allow me to break through to the new Freedom Barrier?

If you're able to overcome these 2 major obstacles, you'll find out very quickly that a coach is one of the key aspects to any successful business or entrepreneur. The difficult step now is to find a coach that suits you, but more importantly, hold you accountable.

As a full time Real Estate Agent and co-owner of a busy Real Estate Investment Club, I understand the challenges that many individuals face. If I could only recommend one coach to everyone I know, hands down it would be Joey Ragona. Joey has been able to successfully analyze these two major aspects, and has helped me get to the next level with the following:

**#1. My personal life**. He was able to identify what was important to me and shape my game plan and strategies to ensure I stayed true to my dreams.

**#2. My business**. By simply asking the right questions and giving me his true undivided attention during scheduled calls, he was able to help me implement the correct solutions to keep the balance between business and personal.

This is where family life and entrepreneurship can collide and Joey sees and understands that. It's an incredible feeling after a call with Joey to be able to feel re-energized and also to have clear direction for the future to accomplish your goals.

So what makes a good coach or mentor? Someone who has also had mentors by some of the best in the industry and is able to share their experiences with you. Joey came from a family of entrepreneurs and through this valuable life experience, he knows what it takes to be successful.

He understands the person you have to become and the skills you have to acquire to go through the rough times. He also knows what you need to do when success comes, in order to continue moving in the right direction.

Since I've been with Joey, my personal life and business have changed for the better. Not because Joey knows everything, but it's because Joey cares. He rewards and recognizes you when you've accomplished the pre-determined goals you've set out. He also, disciplines you and puts you on the spot when you fail to deliver.

There's always hesitation in the beginning... can my coach really deliver? Joey has done that and more. The lessons I've learned have definitely been life changing and that's exactly what I was looking for. Someone to help me keep moving in the right direction and to make me accountable to ensure I took action and to see myself better than I did.

One of my favourite quotes from Joey is to work on "Version 3." What this simply means is, don't try to perfect what you're working on before it's released. Don't strive for perfection, strive for greatness and to do this, find a coach, find Joey.

Thank-you for your guidance and wisdom to allow me to break through the Freedom Barrier.

— *Gary Hibbert*
Real Estate Investor
http://smarthomechoice.ca/

# TODOR YORDANOV

I've never seen anyone implement learned knowledge with the speed and focus as Joey Ragona.

We all take some training here and there, learn few tricks along the way, but my friend Joey takes it to a whole new level with his purpose and near obsession to systemize, utilize, and share everything that he's got.

I remember the first time I spent time in his "classroom" and the "AHA moment" I had when he helped me bring out and define my core values and drive. I still have them on my wall!

Since then he's helped many get clarity in their business and build stronger and better relationships and connections. But most importantly, he helps others to go and find out their WHY!

Why do we do what we do?

A simple question with complicated answers... until you spend some time with him.

— *Todor Yordanov*
Toronto "Legend" Real Estate Investor and Agent
http://www.yordanovteam.com/

# TAHANI ABURANEH

After a talk I had, Joey came up to me to express how inspired he felt in hearing my story (little did I know that I would end up feeling the same way about him soon after). We followed up with a meeting where I got to learn more about Joey. First impression is how humble and amazing of a guy he is.

Later, we end up in the same mastermind group where I really got to know him on a deeper level. I remember one particular plane trip back home — we chatted about business and life and Joey brought many perspectives to the surface I had never "seen" before. He wasn't judgmental about anything...he was just truly honest. And I expected nothing less of him. We laughed, cried and bonded more as friends that day.

For you, reading this book, **you need to know how sincere he is about helping others and making a difference.** He is an incredible friend and an outstanding coach and mentor to many walks of life. When speaking with him or seeing him engaged with his clients, I always leave thinking *"wow, wow, how amazing he is at coaching and how knowledgeable he is at his craft of building businesses that fit people's lives so they can break the freedom barrier".*

If you want to learn from the best, then Joey is the guy. The BONUS is, you get someone who truly wants you to succeed and will challenge you to the core.

Joey is a blessing. And I am so blessed to know him and his wife and I know YOU will be too. Reach out to him and discover for yourself.

Joey, you're a light in this world, keep on shining.

— *Tahani Aburaneh*

International Bestselling Author, Real Estate Trainer and Land Developer
http://www.tahani.ca/

# *STEVE WHITE*

I remember the first time I saw Joey Ragona; it was at a real estate networking seminar and during a break, several hundred people poured out into the lobby for coffee. I was new to the real estate game, had no family or friends who were interested in it so I was pretty well on my own — an introvert among a crowd of confident and successful real estate investors.

Walking through the crowd I passed by a group of about 10 or so that had gathered. At the center was a guy in jeans, a black T-shirt and disheveled hair. Had I not seen his face online or the fact that the group was hanging onto his every word, I would have thought Joey Ragona was the IT guy responsible for ensuring the seminar's PowerPoints ran properly.

I stood on the edge of the group, impressed with what he was saying about how he ran his rental properties, but more so how this unassuming guy held the attention of guys in suits and ties.

I think it was a week or so later I stumbled on Joey's website. I was surprised to find out he was a business coach and specialized in working with real estate investors. I was at my wits end and an emotional wreck trying to get much traction with my investing goals and the free consulting call was priced perfectly.

What was supposed to be a 40-minute overview of where I was in life and career and how Joey could help, ended up being almost two hours of the most honest look at myself I'd probably ever had.

The word "bullshit" was used a lot. Until that point I didn't really know what a life/business coach was for. I realized quickly that they're the people who see in you and what you're doing that you can't see for yourself. I came away from that call probably more deflated that

I was when I started, and was disappointed that I didn't just get an easy answer for a next step.

However, it was what I needed to hear in order to work on myself, my self image, and get clear on my goals before I could make any progress moving forward.

I wish I could say I signed up with Joey right away and things turned around quickly and I'm now a rich, successful real estate investor — but this isn't that kind of story.

I decided to hold off on coaching for a bit, and ended up spending over a year on an emotional roller coaster of moving forward, falling back, gaining weight, getting clear on what I want, losing weight, changing my mind, setting new goals, making gains, separating from my wife and new goals and directions.

Eventually I found my way back to Joey and his community and have found support, advice and clarity helping me and challenging me along the way. I've attended several of his Mastermind groups and weekend seminars and always come away a better person armed with information to make big steps forward.

It's important to point out that things aren't always perfect when working with Joey. He doesn't sugar coat his honesty, though it's certainly not mean or disrespectful. Everyone who works with him is at different stages of their lives and careers. My personal journey was headed in the wrong direction and I'm thankful to Joey for his signposts along the way nudging me onto the right road.

What works for one person or comes easy to them, can be a major challenge to another. There is no "system" that everyone can plug into to achieve success. It's a personal journey and some people need help getting clarity, over fears or past demons.

My investment and mortgage company is a quickly growing success, built on honesty, serving others and targeted relationships, not blanketing houses with useless advertising or gimmicks. I owe a lot of the foundation and future success to Joey Ragona and the skills, clarity and insight he's brought me.

— *Steve White, AMP*
AssetMill.ca
Info@assetmill.ca
Twitter: @assetmill
Facebook: http://facebook.com/AssetMill

## *MAT PICHE*

My journey with Joey Ragona was very insightful and to be honest, life changing!

I know that's an overused cliche´ that you've heard from many late night commercials promising change, but it's the only way I can put it.

Before I began coaching with Joey, my life was chaotic and directionless. I was a full time carpenter breaking my back every day with a dream of becoming a full time real estate agent and investor.

Within a few short months Joey not only taught me about "business" and how to market to my ideal customers effectively but more importantly, he made me look within to get in touch with what's truly important to me.

After digging to uncover my true purpose of why I wanted to be in real estate in the first place is the moment the businesses started to take off!

As entrepreneurs, we often get stuck on the "how-to's". I know I did for the longest time because it's easy to get lost in them. When you're ALWAYS learning new things it feels like you're progressing when in fact, you're really not.

There is a time when the business "tips and tricks" are important for building a successful business; without them we wouldn't have a business at all, but it's not ALL about the strategies as we're often sold by so many "gurus".

I learned your personal life needs the same amount of attention as your business does...and it has to be in some sort of "balance".

This is where the closed group Masterminds really came into effect and why I loved them so much! I always went there expecting to brainstorm some brilliant marketing strategy with the group or share a new idea that would blow them away and grow my business but more often than not, the discussions and coaching quickly became about my personal life as well as everyone else's.

This is where the REAL growth happened for me, and I've witnessed so many others grow along with me.

Joey's able to facilitate the group in a certain way that just made everyone feel safe and open up to each other, even though he's very direct and doesn't sugarcoat anything!

Once everyone got their true priorities in place, the foundation for growth was laid. Then the "tips, tricks and business building strategies" came into play— which were much more effective once we had direction and purpose behind them.

I've witnessed tremendous growth among my peers who sat inside the same coaching program and it was great to see everyone succeeding in their businesses and life.

For me personally, because of his one-on-one guidance, **I was finally able to ditch the hammer and work my own hours as full time realtor and investor.**

This book is full of knowledge to help you take control of your life and I hope you implement it!

*Because of Joey I was able to break MY freedom barrier and have full control of my life and for that, I owe him big!*

— *Mat Piche*
Single-Family Investing Expert/Author
http://www.kwpropertypro.com/
Email: Homes@kwpropertypro.com

# CARLA VIITA

*"BELIEVE in yourself and the will to NO LONGER TOLERATE what doesn't serve you... BUILDS you"* — Joey Ragona

When you have a personal life and business coach/consultant, you will stand to learn from having them by your side, to help you grow areas of your life and business to avoid the pitfalls.

In the last 5 years that I have been sharing, talking and coached by Joey, my business and daily life has been more focused and positive as a result.

With his strategies, recommendations and continuous coaching, Joey has helped me reach clarity and focus on what is important. Of course, I have had some falls and set backs, but Joey was there to help me focus again.

He has helped me bring my confidence back and I know that success leaves clues. Joey has been coached by successful entrepreneurs, such as Greg Habstritt, Eben Pagan, and others that I have personally witnessed become ultra successful in all areas of their lives.

It is a true blessing to witness his success and being a part of it.

Joey's incredible adaptability with people makes him a unique individual because he knows what his clients are seeking before they even know. He does market research, applies his knowledge, tests, and tests again. More than that, he applies what works, and leaves behind what doesn't work.

Repeats the process and I am witnessing business success and growth daily with him and his other coaching clients on a daily basis.

When I met Joey online in 2011, he immediately offered words of wisdom while I was flipping houses to help me find JV investors and find capital for our deals. I applied what I learned and had many successes.

Joey has stood by me in some of the toughest and challenging times...the one that comes to mind is when my partner and I started to build a real estate platform to help us market our homes for sale and rent. After many attempts, obstacles and challenges, I almost gave up...Many times...but we refuse to give up. Joey was there giving me direction and cheering me on.

He has redirected my thinking and getting me to focus on work/life balance. This has helped me a great deal. My problem was I was too scattered in my thinking of who my target market was and is, up until now. He always came back to: *"You need to focus! Who is your customer avatar"?*

A quote from early coaching from Joey that I found in my notes:

*"Focus on your customer avatar, build one out successfully, then repeat the process...if you have to show your customers what they need it will cost you, more time, money and energy. If you give them what they want - you've cut that in half."* — Joey Ragona

And it works in ALL aspects of real estate investing.

Since we serve many different areas of home sellers on our website, that quote reminds me to research and find out what each of those user's problems are, then build those solutions. My new company Flockofhomes.com is in a soft beta launch at the moment while I focus on all sellers to get homes/listings on the website as the "first" step.

I am truly honored and blessed to have met Joey!

Thank you Joey for all you do for other business owners, including myself!

— *Carla Viita*
CoFounder/Owner of Business Development and Marketing
FlockofHomes.com

# PIERRE-PAUL TURGEON

I feel very lucky to have come across Joey Ragona as a coach in my real estate business and in my life. Over the years, he has helped me tremendously in solving many challenges in developing my business from scratch after I left my cushy, six-figure salary job with CMHC as a multifamily underwriter.

For many years I was like a deer in headlights in a permanent state of fear about how I was going to make a living and support my family.

Starting a new business with no prior experience turned out to be even harder than I could have imagined and Joey was there for me during those difficult times to provide me sound advice, such as technical tips on how to structure my website, and ideas on the type of content I needed to make the site more appealing.

He was also very instrumental in assisting me in developing the right entrepreneurial frame of mind to succeed and to ensure I place the focus on my clients' needs above anything else.

His advice has always been spot on and he has never hesitated to challenge me on my limiting beliefs and to push me beyond to my full potential. He'll call a spade a spade and will not accept any B.S. from his clients while at the same remaining respectful and non-judgmental.

It is a joy to work with Joey Ragona!

— *Pierre-Paul Turgeon*
Canada's Leading Authority for investing in apartment Buildings
http://www.multifamilyblueprint.com/

# *WAYNE DOLSON*

"REAL-RAW-AND-TRUTH" — this is how Joey coaches. I met Joey in 2011 when I attended one of his Mastermind all day sessions. I had been in the retail industry for 23-years up to that point and a real estate investor in Lease-to-Own deals since 2009.

However, my desire not to work for someone else had been high for a while.

However, when you get into a comfortable state being paid well and able to provide things for your family it is hard to get out. After my first of many Masterminds with Joey I could see the passion this once DJ turned successful entrepreneur had to help others and see that there is more.

Joey's style of coaching is not for the faint of heart. He's not there to be your friend. Well, this is what he says, however as I have gotten to know Joey over the years, raw-real and truthful as he is, he is a friend. A friend who will tell you straight up if you're being an ass or not. Joey helps dig with you deep down to find the real YOU. To me this is what makes for a better coach. Someone who does care like a friend that you see clearly on what it is you need to do with your life.

I have sat in many of Joey's Mastermind sessions where he truly shows how he gets to the heart of what it is someone is seeking. *Joey just isn't a coach for real estate investors, he is a coach of humans.*

Even though I invest part time, I know that being a FULL TIME real estate investor running from deal to deal is not my thing. For me it is about making my money work for me. When I started my corporation in 2009 I had the vision of being just that a full time investor — just like "everyone else".

Over the years with words and advice from Joey, I have seen that my calling isn't to be a full time investor, but to use real estate as another stream of income so I can do what I truly am meant to do.

Joey's rawness is what truly helps an individual see what it is they are meant to be doing with their life. I know I am destined to help others in many faucets of their life. I am someone who likes to help.

Although I have yet to eliminate my position in "WORKING FOR THE MAN" as of yet, Joey's words stay with me daily. I continue to take in what he says using it to map out the next go of my life.

I will attend and support Joey with his purpose and cause. As a student I am a believer and one-day hope to help so many others in a raw, real and truthful way just like my friend and mentor Joey Ragona.

In closing, life is short. We take time for granted and the remaining time is yours. You need to search for it, embrace it, and drive it forward so you can excel at more in life. If you ever step into choosing Joey as your guide in this life, I am certain you will find who and what you are.

RAW, REAL, and TRUTH

— *Wayne Dolson*
Senior-Partner/President
MTM-Investment Group Inc.

# LINDSAY R. ALLISON

If you haven't met Joey before — you need to.

We are all living within our own story. What is it that you are telling yourself every day?

Joey has this uncanny ability to help you clear away your mental noise. His "no bullshit" approach allows you to get better acquainted with yourself (especially with the parts of yourself you don't want to see!).

Before I met Joey, I was trapped in a world where my mental picture was keeping myself, and my business, in a standstill. I quickly realized that I had a foundation for my physical business world, but not for my digital business world. I had no idea that this "missing link" was such a crucial step in getting to the life I FULLY want to live.

As soon as I started to implement Joey's strategies, I began to feel less stressed and more in control. Once I became completely aligned with my purpose, the path to success became simple.

Joey simplifies things so you can cut the crap.

Just imagine the lifestyle that is your own freedom. Imagine how this will become possible by implementing the foundations you learn in this book.

Keep this book close to you, for it may be one of the most valuable tools you come across. If you're ready to face your own challenges head on, congratulations. Be prepared for the ride of your life!

— *Lindsay R. Allison*
Award-Winning Author, Writer
Content Writing, Book Creation
www.lindsayrallison.com

# Introduction

## DON'T Skip This...

You're holding what I believe is the most powerful book you will ever read about real estate investing.

Because rather than being another copy-cat "HOW-TO" about real estate investing, this is a "WHY" and "WHAT" book about FREEDOM, and the LIFESTYLE you want to achieve from your real estate.

But there's a problem —

Even though I meet people, week after week, who tell me they want freedom from real estate investing, most of them actually GIVE UP more freedom than they GAIN.

In my mind, that's counter intuitive.

They sit in seminars, workshops, and trainings — writing notes, and "networking"...

But they AREN'T buying properties.

Why?

Because there's too much too learn. There's a lot of information, and they don't know which real estate model is best.

So many feel like they're getting nowhere, even though they're putting all they got into it, week after week.

They aren't buying because they're afraid something might go wrong, or that they can't pay the bills, or worried that they'll lose money and go bankrupt.

Sometimes it goes even deeper — they're afraid of making a mistake, alienating friends and family because they failed. So they want things done RIGHT the first time.

It's plain and simple: they have a fear of failure; a lack of belief in themselves.

They are trying to quiet their mind to deal with the fear...

And it's an epidemic among people interested in real estate investing.

That's one of the reasons why I wrote this book — to help you overcome whatever fear you might have, so you can apply the knowledge you gather inside those workshops and seminars.

I thought long and hard about the topic of this book, and even started writing different ideas that ended up being my version of another "how-to" real estate book. But this didn't feel right to me because even though you'll read HOW I do things, this is not about me. It's about you.

Perhaps you want more "me" time and flexibility. It's great to want a flow of money coming in, but without a solid plan or direction, you could end up spinning your wheels.

If you want to get out of the rat race...the 9-5...it's best to retain as much as possible from the words in this book.

In fact, don't read this book...**memorize it**.

*Because it will change the way you think about real estate investing.*

It will change the way you think about freedom.

This book will allow you to become a far more skilled — and successful — real estate investor.

It does all of this by giving you a simple strategic framework to fit ANY real estate model INTO your LIFE.

So it's not a book of "mechanics" or "strategies".

Yet, it will reveal THE ultimate strategy to fit the right real estate into YOUR life.

It's a book of reality, experience, challenges, and encouragement.

This is my gift to you.

Come back to this book time and time again when you fall off track, become overwhelmed, or lose focus on your true end goal.

This is not about real estate investing.

It's about how real estate investing fits your LIFE.

## What to Expect from This Book

I'm not here to waste your time with fluff. I wrote this book for one simple reason: to help you achieve YOUR freedom.

I know that's a huge undertaking because every other real estate book promises the same thing, but I'm going to clear out the crap from the concepts and common problems, and deliver the inner game of real estate investing success.

We're going to get right down to business with the framework I have been teaching to my high-level coaching clients for years that will also get YOU moving in the right direction in building your real estate business.

You'll begin the process of rewiring your mindset to see *your* version of success in a totally new, effective way.

I have to warn you though — this book is raw and real. I'm not pretending to be THE real estate "guru". And I'm not going to apologize for the direct approach I have to my writing or teaching. I care about serving the people who will connect with my message.

I'm okay if I don't win a popularity contest with the entire real estate investing community with my thoughts, theories, concepts, opinions, ideas, methods, strategies and whatever else is in this book.

I could care less about winning an award, either. *I simply wanted to write a book that captures who I am every day with my coaching clients* — a book that I'm proud to have out there.

That being said...I would LOVE your feedback, if you care to let me know. More importantly, my wish is that you DO something with it NOW.

Because my "job" as a real estate investor business coach is to help people use the real estate fundamentals they're already learning in their business, the right way.

## Who This Is NOT For...

Before we get any further, I want to give you a summary of what this book is NOT about. So that you don't waste your time.

I didn't write a book to teach you about the different real estate investment strategies such as:

- Buy and hold
- Wholesaling
- Flipping
- Rent to Own
- Joint Venture
- Etc.

Why? Simply because there's no shortage of books and training already out there that are great at teaching investment strategies.

At the end of this book, however, I'll give you my highest recommendations so you can dive further into your niche...after we FIND it here, together!!!

Exciting, right?

Because the SOLE purpose of this book is to *get you moving*.

The ideal person who will benefit from this book is someone who is trapped inside the fear of moving ahead.

And the strategy you'll learn from this book is one that will apply to ANY one of the real estate investment strategies out there.

So, if you are:

- Looking for a fast, easy way to get rich in real estate
- Searching for "creative ways" to do real estate investing
- Wanting another "how-to invest" in real estate book

This ISN'T for you.

You might be thinking, *"If this doesn't teach me HOW to buy real estate, why do I need it?"*

**This book IS intended to help you build your real estate business so you can enjoy all the freedom you deserve, without giving up your life to do it.**

I'm going to share what I've learned since 2008 when I bought my first property and, over the last 6 years coaching, training, and speaking with other real estate investors.

This book is written for the person who wants to have more freedom *while they're investing in real estate.*

Read the above sentence again...because <u>it's not a trade-off</u>. It's NOT about "WHEN I get [X], I'll have [Y]".

It's about *designing* your real estate business with your lifestyle TODAY as priority, and your lifestyle tomorrow as the goal.

## This is NOT a "Get Rich Quick"

Most of the people I meet want to make fast money in real estate. They've been seduced by HGTV flip shows, thinking they need to own 50 or 100 properties, or something crazy like that.

There is a BUSINESS side of real estate investing that so many people overlook. It's one of the main reasons I started coaching real estate investors...because many get caught up in the world of fantasy to make 5-10 thousand dollars of passive cash flow, replace their income, quit their job, and travel the world.

If you're like most of the students and clients I've had, you're probably nodding your head thinking *"Yeah...what's wrong with that?"*

Absolutely nothing's wrong with it.

But you have to set your real estate investing up as a business from day one.

And as with every business, there's a learning curve, adjustments, growth, dips, obstacles, pivots, and more.

And that all takes TIME — the four-letter word that many real estate investors HATE to hear.

## How to Use This Book

To make this an effective read, here are a few suggestions on how to use this book to your ultimate advantage.

**Here's what you do:**

1. **Create a "book journal"**. Meaning, write down notes and ideas that you get from this book. I know you can just highlight sections and return to it anytime, but something is more powerful when you write things down in your own handwriting.

2. **Play along.** At times throughout this book, I'll ask you to write things down — mostly about what you're thinking. There's no right or wrong answers, and you'll benefit from recording this stuff in your book journal because you can go back a few months from now to check out how far you've actually progressed.

3. **Highlight the most significant parts of the book that have impacted you.** When you DO need to come back and scan through whatever inspired you, the highlights will help you find what you're looking for.

4. **Scan through the book quickly first.** I've laid the chapters and sections out in small chunks so you can get to what you want to learn quickly. A lot of people think they need to pick up a book and start reading from page one to the last page. The fastest way to get through a book is to pre-scan the entire book so your subconscious mind absorbs information without you even realizing it. When you go back to read it, you'll see that your comprehension is better.

I recommend you re-read this book several times during the next few weeks. With each reading, new "secrets" will be revealed to you.

## My Disclaimer

As you'll experience throughout this book, I'm a straight shooter. I've got nothing to hide in my intentions for writing this book.

There's no secret that I'm a business coach and I charge people to help them build their business.

Above all, I created this book to spread my message, raise my voice, and share what I've learned throughout my own experiences — which includes coaching and training hundreds of real estate investors.

There's no doubt in my mind that someone will see this book as a "self-promotion business card" — but it's far from it. The way I see it, there's no better way to help you move from fear to *actually doing something in your life* without PROVING to you that others have done it. I Intend to do just that with social proof, and examples from my coaching and training with real estate entrepreneurs.

A couple of years ago, another real estate author subtly "called me out" in her book (not actually using my name, of course — so there's a chance I could totally be wrong, and I don't want to judge...but I just had this inner gut feeling!) — from the context of the chapter, it was pretty clear it was directed at me. She wrote that my "intentions" of responding to questions in real estate forums was to only to get coaching clients.

As of the time of this writing, this person has never attended any of my events, Masterminds, or has ever seen me speak. If she had, maybe she would understand the passion and purpose behind my "intentions".

I understand I'll never get 100% of the popularity vote...and that's cool. I respect everyone's opinion.

Of COURSE I wanted business — who's hiding that? Let's be real, **everyone** has something to sell. Including me, AND that author. If you think people are writing books, creating seminars, webinars, and inventing programs without the intention of selling them, you're living in a fog.

The days of subtle sales and trickery are long gone.

While we're on the subject, I ALSO wrote this book to build more authority and get more leads that will hopefully turn into customers, and buy some of my awesome programs that will change their life.

Because I help people by *actually* showing them the value of what I do. It's my "big secret" for attracting clients.

But if all you get from this book is that swift kick in the ass to do something you've never done...my "job" is complete. All I ask is that you let me know. Email me. Put a "thank you" on my Facebook Page, send me a Tweet...whatever.

Finally, I wrote this book because I'm a coach and can totally help you on a personal basis if you so choose to ask me about it.

I think that's transparent enough, don't you?

# What You'll Learn

Inside these pages are valuable lessons learned from experiences that would take years for you to discover on your own.

I've coached enough real estate entrepreneurs to have a good sense about your personal challenges, fears, and obstacles.

Listening to their stories, struggles, pains, frustrations, wants, and needs — I knew in my heart that this book needed to be different than any other one out there.

I'm giving you a *framework* from which to hang your own personality, skills, and style so you can avoid many of the common traps — and help you push through your fears to actually *doing something* to change your life.

If you're still reading this after the **"Who This Is NOT For..."** section, I'm guessing you're in one of 2 categories:

1) You have a full time job and want to buy real estate so you can quit your job and live from the cash flow of your properties.

2) You already OWN real estate, and have found out that you've added more chaos to your life, where the ,"business" is stealing the very freedom you were after in the first place.

**Either way, you're going to win from reading this book.**

Even though this is not a book that will teach you the mechanics of buying real estate, you're still going to learn my *Hypersonic Investment Strategy*™ to help you reach your first investment property as fast as possible.

## Introduction to the Framework

I told you we would waste no time.

Before we look at a few important pieces of the puzzle, I want to share the *Hypersonic Investment Strategy*™

**Here it is:**

**1:** Investment strategy

**2-4:** Investment groups, meet-ups, mentors, and/or coaches

**5-6**: Books and programs per year

**7-9:** Months of research

**10:** Hours per week

Simple. IF you follow that, you should have your first investment property within a year.

No wasting time…and, you'll be well prepared for your new business adventure; adjusting and dealing with most of the stuff that will inevitably pop up along the way.

Here's an important note about the framework before we dive in: if you're wondering, *"What's first?"* — well, there isn't any "first". That's the magic of this framework.

Even if you're a bit in a fog right now about what I'm saying, that's cool. It'll all come together when we dive deep into each piece of the framework later on.

*"Trust the process…"* I always say to my clients…

## Why I'm Qualified to Write This Book

One of the first things you should know about me is that **I'm not a real estate "guru".**

I DON'T "live, breathe and sleep" real estate (as they always say).

Quite the opposite.

But that doesn't mean I don't do well.

I'll admit right up front — I DON'T have hundreds of properties, or 50 joint venture investors.

That's because *I don't want them.*

I figured out early on that chasing someone else's real estate dream just added more chaos into my life. I was listening to other people WAY too much in the beginning — thinking I wanted the same thing.

Once I understood exactly what I was looking real estate to do FOR me, my business and life changed dramatically.

You're not going to hear me say something like, *"Just do what I did so you can be like me."* You WILL hear me encourage, challenge, suggest, and push you to follow my framework.

Because since 2008, I've built my real estate business to practically run on autopilot using this exact framework.

In 2011, I set out to focus on helping other real estate investors by personally coaching them through their obstacles and fears...again, utilizing the framework I'm going to show you right here.

From that time on, I've trained and coached hundreds of real estate investors, probably like you, who:

- Are in jobs they hate
- Have large debt
- Have a major attachment to money
- Lack confidence, motivation, are unsure of themselves
- Have little to no business or marketing knowledge
- Don't know where they're going
- Are results-only oriented
- Wear to many hats trying to balance friends, family, job, real estate portfolio/education, spouse
- Have marital tension because it's challenging to get their spouse on board

Does any of that sound like you?

I'm guessing some of it does, or you wouldn't be reading this.

If you're totally brand new, I know how you feel. I felt the exact same sense of being overwhelmed that you might have right now. I discovered really quickly that the fundamentals of real estate don't change all that often — and by that, I mean never.

Like you, I went to the professionals to learn the proper, sophisticated fundamentals of investing in real estate. Wherever you are now in your real estate business, believe me when I say the fundamentals and mechanics are easy.

I don't know enough about the different types of real estate niches to be comfortable teaching them. I'll leave that to the experts.

What I AM very comfortable teaching is how to take all of that information you're learning, strip out the nonsense, and help you apply the most important parts to build your real estate business.

There **are** fundamentals of real estate you will need to follow — but for this book, I'm going to show you a *framework* I call the *Hypersonic Investment Strategy*™ to get you going.

In fact, it's a framework that you can apply to just about ANY real estate investment niche you choose.

In other words, it adapts to YOU.

This book is about living your life TODAY — right NOW.

It's about *setting your freedom* up from day ONE.

There's NO REASON to *wait* for freedom!

# The Clock Is Ticking

In this book you're going to learn how to win the inner game of having a successful real estate business — A.K.A. the strategies that are the make-up of successful real estate entrepreneurs, and how they master their businesses and their lives.

I don't know about you, but in the past 5 years, the world has been speeding up all around me.

Things are coming at me faster than ever before.

And time is also flying by.

I don't see the world slowing down anytime soon, and neither is the time in which I have to achieve what I want.

From the conversations I have with people every week, the haunting pain of regret for not doing something is a big issue.

Rather than give you *another retake* on the *mechanics* of real estate investing, I'm providing the game plan, encouragement, and ammunition to help you move forward through the wall of fear and doubt with every ounce of willpower you have.

Here's why:

There are tons of people out there with the real estate knowledge. They understand the mechanics and strategies, yet they're still broke.

They're still working full time, dreading the commute back and forth to work, and the only thing they look forward to is the 2-day weekend break from being ground down every day...that is, until they have to do it all over again.

They've turned to real estate investing for a way out.

But they're still not out. They haven't even started. If they have started, they're stuck.

## The 5-Year "Plan"

EVERYONE wants the perfect real estate investing plan.

I've found that most people have no trouble dreaming about their future. But when it comes to their present life, it's difficult for them to move past their fears.

So they *reset* their 5-year mark just about **every** year.

For instance, someone will tell me in 2016 they want to quit their job in 5 years (2021).

Great.

For the next 12 months, they do NOTHING.

They're "learning" — going to seminars and workshops.

So when 2017 rolls around, they'll tell me about their 5-year plan **again**. Which is now unrecognized to them...RESET to 2022.

In reality, they have 4 years left because they've USED UP a year procrastinating/learning, whatever the reason.

There's no DO-OVER...we can't "reset" a part of our lives because we didn't like what we did. The time is GONE.

This making sense?

So my job as a coach is not to tell you, *"It's okay..."* It's to remove your blinders and hit you with a dose of reality.

## 12-Month Immediate Goal

5-year goals are great, but it's too far into the future. It allows us to delay immediate action because we feel we've "got some time".

That's why I ask my clients for their 12-month **immediate** goals. Stuff they MUST do *this* year.

I don't really care about 5-years from now. I care about what you're doing NOW to GET you to your 5-year goal.

If you're sitting in seminar rooms "learning", I'm sorry to say it, you're not DOING. Learning is not *doing*.

You can easily get caught up in the research to make sure everything is "just right".

Let's focus on the 12-month plan here.

## Goals Are Not Meant to Achieve

I also want to make a point about goals for a moment.

Goals are not really meant to achieve...they are meant to make you MOVE.

In other words, if you don't HIT a particular goal in the time you've set, it's REALLY OKAY.

Focus on how far you've PROGRESSED.

Because if you didn't set the goal in the first place, you would probably stand still and NEVER move — am I right?

When I was writing this book, I missed my "deadline" twice. It didn't discourage me because I looked at how much I had written, and I just pushed the deadline a week further each time.

Does that indicate that I'm not successful, or productive?

If I sat on my ass doing nothing and let the deadline pass, then maybe...but that's not what happened.

So the same goes for you. Your 5-year plan, how many properties you own, whether you quit your job or not...as LONG as you're progressing, it's the most important thing!

We tend to get caught up in RESULTS-ONLY mode; *which means we think we're productive or successful only when we achieve.*

If your goal was to lose 10 pounds in 2 months, but you only lost 5 pounds, would you stop? Would you tell people you were unsuccessful?

Sadly, some do.

But I wouldn't. I would congratulate myself on the journey and understand that I may have overestimated, or maybe I didn't follow my diet, or something else threw me off course...whatever.

## Case Study: The Busy Badge of Honour

This book is about sharing my personal belief of living a stress-free life TODAY while building a real estate business.

I'm not out there, bouncing around, looking for real estate deals 24-7.

I have developed a system that works for just about *any niche* and real estate model — mainly because I've found so many real estate investors stuck in the learning trap.

I started hand holding and coaching real estate investors to help them move past the wall of fear and grow their businesses.

One of my coaching clients Monika (who you've met at the beginning of this book) hired me because I brought some of those lifestyle oversights to her attention.

I remember the Mastermind session like it was yesterday. She thought the busier she was, the more successful she was.

I told her she was wearing the "busy badge of honour" and it only fed her ego, while it slowly eroded everything she said she cared about: primarily, her kids and her family.

I intuitively decided that she needed to see her life in a REAL, visual way. So I spent about 25 minutes writing down every minute of her day on a huge piece of paper.

The more I added, the more embarrassed she became.

There was literally no room for *anything* in her day.

She was "busy", but there was no room for error.

And certainly no room for her to be a mom and a wife, even though it was "scheduled" in.

I asked her, *"Can you point to where you're spending quality time with your kids?"*

She pointed to one part of her day that read, *"Kids home from school 3pm-3:20pm."*

And then to another part that read, *"Dinner 6pm-6:30pm."*

I asked her, *"Great, so that means your cell phone is off and you're totally engaged with them?"*

*"Oh, no...I can't turn the phone off, that's the source of my business"*, she told me.

*"But you're telling me you're ENGAGED in quality time with your kids in those time slots, right?"* I subtly challenged.

*"Yes"* she confirmed.

*"Can anyone say delusional?"* I asked the group.

Yeah — I'm that blunt. Because I've got no time to waste with anyone. If I would have let her off and tell her, *"Okay, then, if it works for you..."* I firmly believe she would not have changed her life in the same way she has, since I've been working with her. (Talk about a GREAT plug for my coaching huh?)

The MORE she added to her plate, the LESS freedom she had.

Even though she was physically there with her kids and her husband at night, **the business consumed her**.

IT (the business) was first. When the phone rang, it was, *"Hang on, honey, I've got to take this."*

If she was at her kids' sports games, she'd be *catching up* on emails.

REALLY?

Does that sound like engagement to you? Head down, buried in a 5.6-inch screen?

It may sound a bit harsh after reading the story, but it's the truth. And we are ALL guilty of this.

I'm not telling you anything she doesn't already know. Like I said, you've met her at the beginning of this book where she's told the story in her own words.

So — let's be REALLY clear about YOUR *freedom* part so you do NOT give up your current life!

We have to roll up our sleeves and get to work...

# PART I

# CHAPTER 1

## What Do I Need To Know First?

Sadly, there are too many real estate entrepreneurs stuck in the learning trap.

They are always learning, but never achieving.

It's a very profitable trap for seminars, courses, and real estate "gurus" with a primary goal to keep more passive income flying into their bank accounts.

I don't believe ALL of them are like this, but I'm sure you'll agree there are a LOT MORE taking our money while declaring false promises, than there are people truly attempting to help.

So I want to stop the feeding frenzy of crooks that have no moral fiber, as they destroy peoples lives.

That might sound harsh, but it's most important to me to raise my voice and spread my message because I've met people who have literally lost their life savings, their homes, relationships, marriages, and so on because of some "guru" who could care less about anyone.

Their primary goal is about their bank account. I really cannot fathom stealing someone's life savings just so they'll "buy my program".

## Are You Committed or Just Interested?

One of my first coaches, Greg Habstritt, looked at me and said, *"...maybe that's why you are where you are...I'm not saying it's bad — I'm not saying it's good — I'm saying it just is."*

He was pointing out that I was unwilling to commit to change; reluctant to try something new to move me forward.

If we want to get a different outcome from what we have now, then we have to change what we're doing every day, right?

It truly comes down to what we are comfortable doing. When we are uncomfortable, we'll pull back and want to return to our "safe zone".

As John Assaraf says, *"There are two types of people in the world: those INTERESTED in success, and those who are COMMITTED to it."*

That one quote has become an important part of who I am and how I move forward in my real estate investing.

If you asked me, I would say that MOST people are just *interested* in real estate investing. They are *interested* in a better life, more money, quitting their job, and having all the free time to do what they love.

They're doing **whatever is convenient.**

But if you're committed, **you'll do whatever it takes.**

A word of warning though...I've coached many people who are "willing to do whatever it takes", even if it means sacrificing parts of their lives to do it.

And THIS IS A MAJOR PROBLEM.

There's no reason to sacrifice anything.

I've learned this from first-hand experience.

So rather than have you sacrifice, let's get you strategically committed, okay?

## Are You Like These Investors?

Like I've mentioned, I've spent the last several years with a considerable number of real estate investors — both experienced and newbies — so I think I have a good handle on what most of them want.

By asking them this simple question: *"What ONE thing would improve your life the most?"* I'll get a variety of responses, but it all sums up to these TOP three:

- More Money/Financial Independence
- More Freedom and Flexibility/Quit my Job/ Quality Time with my Family
- Travel the world

If those answers resonate with you, I'm not surprised. It's what we ALL want.

But here's what I figured out:

Most of these investors lack focus. Even the experienced ones.

What I mean is they spend so much time — sometimes YEARS — carefully weighing the pros and cons, deciding which real estate model is the BEST so they avoid making a mistake.

I get it. Most investors are very analytical people. They want things done right the first time. Yet, they're impatient when things don't happen quickly enough. A lot of them are struggling with confidence and energy to move forward.

How do I know this?

Because these (and more) are the commonalities of my coaching clients.

It doesn't surprise me when somebody tells me they *"haven't yet decided"*...

When I started attending the real estate club I'm involved with, I sat amongst people who told me they were "still looking"...and it's been 2 or 3 years!

Everyone's different, I understand, but these are the same people who are impatient, want freedom more than ever and can't wait to get out of their shitty day job.

What's wrong with that picture?

I finally discovered a commonality amongst most of the people I met. They lacked business experience. They had to constantly be reminded to "run real estate like a business". I quickly found that this wasn't common sense for a lot of people.

I'm not any smarter than they are. I do though, have a bit of a head start in this area because I've grown up in an entrepreneurial family — so business is second nature to me.

However, most people in real estate are investing for one reason — to quit their job. This is cool, but it also creates a lot of *overwhelm* and stress in their lives because there's just too much information. They don't know which real estate model is best, and things aren't happening fast enough for them.

One of the strengths I bring to the real estate investing table is the different mindset than most who have never owned businesses. Too many investors lose focus and direction, and don't have a clear plan in order to spend time and money effectively.

## 2 Major Groups of Investors

With the risk of insulting you — in my experience, there are 2 clear-cut groups of investors.

Actually, there are 3 — the third minority group is filled with those who know exactly what they want real estate to do, and begin building it from the start as a business.

But let's focus on those 2 other groups because this is where I've found MOST investors usually living:

**Group 1. The Dreamers and Draggers** — the people who go to seminars, meet-ups, networking groups, and workshops, read all the books, and NEVER buy a property because there's always "something missing." In other words, they're dragging their feet. They are the *majority*, and we'll talk more about this group later.

**Group 2. The Eager Enthusiasts (Over-Zealous)** — the people who are so fed up with their lives, jobs, financial status, and so on — they want a CHANGE, RIGHT NOW. They're so fed up that they employ the *fast and furious* approach and start buying up every opportunity in sight because they want the immediate results. So they assume that the faster they go, the faster they can stop the pain.

Although these people ARE action takers, they're usually adding more chaos to their lives because they have no plan, no direction, and very little or no business experience. Money is usually the primary motivator for them.

Group 2 are the people I usually work with, primarily because they don't have business experience and lose focus pretty quickly.

They're VERY distracted, and they're in pain. They have emotional pain.

And like I said, because they want to subdue the pain so quickly, they give up the very thing they're after: *lifestyle and freedom* — because they're trying to piece together a real estate investing business by acquiring everything they can, as fast as possible. They usually chase every opportunity that sounds like it will get them out of their personal hell.

By working with these real estate investors over the years, I've learned what they need to help them succeed in real estate investing. In hearing their struggles week in and week out, I've uncovered the top challenges real estate investors have.

And this book is the result of understanding and working through their struggles and challenges.

It's been a long road to get to this point, through my own personal journey and walking the path with others just like you.

## What Group Are You In?

I've mentioned the 2 distinct groups of real estate investors. They are my own definition — it's nothing official:

The **Dreamers and Draggers,** and the **Eager Enthusiasts**.

The third group is what I call the Strategic group. This group is filled with people who *usually* have a business background, OR they come into real estate investing with an alternative goal other than just "making money."

Their r*eason, purpose,* and *approach* to real estate investing is slightly different from the 2 other groups.

That is where I sit.

Please don't think I'm saying I'm better than you, or anyone else. We are all equal — we just have different experiences, learn differently, and understand different things. I'm just pointing out that I see real estate investing as it truly is:

**A business that compliments BOTH my lifestyles. It aligns with my *today* lifestyle, and funds my *tomorrow lifestyle*.**

More importantly, it's a business that will NOT *take away* my freedom, but give me MORE of it.

Let's face it — Group 1, the Dreamers and Draggers, are more than likely staying exactly where they are. You know what I'm talking about here, because I'll bet you know people like this.

They will tell you what they dream about and how great it would be "if only".

Bottom line:

*We always do what we believe is important.* The proof is in our daily actions. That's why you can pinpoint people who are dreamers. They are doing the same thing over and over again and never really moving anywhere...but they're great at complaining, wishing, dreaming, and hoping.

I find that most real estate entrepreneurs who are trapped, stuck, and fearful, constantly asking the "what ifs" stay living in mediocrity LONGER than they need to. It's like a huge hamster wheel, constantly spinning, with limiting questions and justifications.

So where are **you** right now?

Which group do you fit in with?

If you ARE in Group 1, and you can admit that you've spent enough time "researching", hoping, and praying, then I'm honoured you found me and discovered this book, so I can move you OUT of that group.

If you're in Group 2, then by now you've realized there's something amiss with your real estate investment business, and you need help getting your focus back.

If you're in Group 3, you're probably already aware of what I'm talking about here, and just want some really cool ways to turn up the performance of your business.

Whichever the reason or the group you fit into, you're going to get major value from this book.

# CHAPTER 2

## How Do I Get What I Want?

I don't know very many people who DON'T want more money.

It's pretty safe to say the objective of investing in real estate is to make money.

There's nothing wrong with that target — but the problem is, it's the ONLY target for a LOT of people.

Sadly, this is an area where I find many real estate entrepreneurs are lacking. Their *belief* in what they are trying to achieve is usually fueled only from some sort of material gain. Their freedom is measured by how much money they will make per month.

The problem with thinking on a material level is that once a "storm" hits (and it will), many of us tend to look for other avenues to get the results we're looking for faster. And that keeps us spinning our wheels.

## The 80/20 Rule About Real Estate

I really believe we need a new approach to real estate investing. You may have heard about the 80/20 rule before, and it's great to apply to your real estate investing business.

*The Pareto Principle* states that roughly 80% of your results come from 20% of your effort.

If the Dreamers and Draggers followed this rule just to **get IN the game**, they would be so much further ahead.

The same goes for the Eager Enthusiasts. If they used this rule to build out what works so they CAN expand later, they would not be spinning their wheels every day.

The benefit of understanding this rule is so important to grasp if you want to build a business successfully, because the Pareto Principle is a *universal law* that applies to almost every aspect of our lives.

To give you an example of how the 80/20 rule works in real estate, it means that basically 80% of your wealth comes from only 20% of your investments.

The other investments (whatever they are) are just *okay*.

Here's another example:

When I do a live demonstration in a room full of real estate investors to prove the 80/20 rule, I'll begin by asking the entire room to stand up.

Every time, the room is occupied with either 20% of women and 80% of men, or vice versa.

Of course, it's not EXACT...but it's close enough.

Try this little experiment the next time you're at a real estate event. Take a look around the room to see the 80/20 rule in effect.

Alright, so what does this have to do with you making money in real estate?

Remember, 80% of your results are going to come from 20% of what you *focus* on.

This means that 80% of your *greatest* cash flow is going to come from 20% of your properties.

It also means that 80% of your properties will be tenanted, on average. The other 20% of your properties will be in tenant turnover, or vacant.

Keep this in mind as you begin to build your business and your strategies, because if you have nothing in place to deal with vacancies, or the "other 20%" you're going to run into trouble really fast.

It's great to have 100% of your properties rented...but always leave room for that 20%.

Let's continue:

80% of your maintenance, problems and challenges — including tenant issues — will come from 20% of your properties.

It doesn't mean the other 80% are perfect; it just means there will more than likely be about 20% of your properties that REALLY stand out.

# The 80/20 Rule For the Real Estate Investor

Okay — here's where the shit gets real.

80% of people reading this won't do *anything* with the information, ideas, advice, strategies, or methods in here.

They'll nod their head a few times, and then move on to the next book.

Or worse: they won't even READ the entire thing.

They'll get to Chapter 1 and never pick it up again.

But it also means that the 20% left over from those 80% are going *start* to take action...and I honour that!

I can't predict who the 80% or who the 20% are, personally, I'm just hoping you're in that 20%.

Being in the 20% has nothing to do with your experience, education, financial status, colour, race, or anything along those lines.

It has everything to do with your level of *true commitment*.

Here's the next dosage of reality:

FROM those 20% of action takers, 80% of those people will STOP in their tracks as they hit the first obstacles.

That doesn't leave many that actually move on to do something, does it?

That's also another layer of what this book is all about: it's about sifting through the 80% and getting this message to the 20% that are going to do something TODAY and KEEP GOING.

# CHAPTER 3

## What Are The Traps, Truths and Tricks in Real Estate Investing?

I'll be the first to tell you that real estate investing has saved my future. I am totally grateful for the people I've met and learned from.

In EVERY industry, there are 2 sides. The "dark side", and the "light side".

On the reverse side of the coin (the "dark side"), I'm not afraid to admit that I'm disgusted with some people within the industry who are lying and stealing from regular people — people like you and I who just want a better life.

I've witnessed too many real estate seminars and workshops where the claim is, *"Everything will be perfect if you just follow my lead."*

And when we don't, we'll get the guilt line: *"What, you don't want to make $100K in [insert "guru" program here]?"*

It's VERY easy to sell a dream and an idea to someone who is at their wits end. The more pain someone is in, the easier it is to sell this person an apparent solution. And if you're a good salesperson, it's like shooting fish in a barrel.

It's a sad fact that I've met people who have actually lost their entire savings, retirement funds, and even PERSONAL homes to liars.

Just be aware that there are some really smooth players out there who put on a mask to walk among the "light side", but are only truly interested in lining their own pockets with other people's hard earned savings.

And they don't really care HOW they do it.

I'm never going to claim that I'm 100% right. Throughout this book you'll find MANY of my personal opinions because I'm writing from my heart and my experience after listening to countless people's stories.

You can agree or disagree with me as you read it...it's your choice. I'm just letting you know what I've witnessed.

## The Truth About the Real Estate Investing Industry

The truth (as I see it) about the real estate investing industry is that it's great in promising fast wealth.

Quick riches and "creative" ways to make money are the top Google searches for real estate.

There's no shortage of television shows, seminars, meet-ups, workshops, books, and home study courses that are selling us exactly what we want — FAST CASH with NO MONEY needed that gets us MASSIVE FREEDOM so we can live on a beach for the rest of our lives.

This is just not true.

I trust that I'm approaching real estate investing a helluva lot different than most people. Again, I'm not better, just looking at things in a new light.

I'm a witness of the state of the real estate investing industry, and I'm currently not impressed by what's out there...for the most part.

I've met people who's lives have been totally shattered and ripped apart by real estate "gurus" who are promising the world.

You may be thinking, *"Joey, there's corruption everywhere, in every business."* And you'd be right. But real estate investing has to be one of the most tainted, in my opinion.

However, people are getting smarter. They are becoming more educated. Thanks to the way we are connected in this world, it's very difficult for someone to hide anymore — especially if you're objective is about ripping people off.

But there are still "gurus" flying just under the radar out there selling people on **false hopes and dreams**.

And they'll blame the real estate investor for "not taking proper action" when it fails.

Even though a lot of times it IS true (which we'll cover A LOT about in this book), MOST people are overwhelmed with information, and are looking at real estate investing through rose-colored glasses.

By now, you might think I'm against real estate investing considering how I've been referring to everything...

...But that's the furthest from the truth.

All you need is a strategic plan on how to invest in real estate with the knowledge you have, or going to have.

## The Cash Flow Myth

Let's start with the biggest myth of all.

For years I've been speaking on stages and in seminar rooms busting the myth that people have become "rich" by living from their cash flow.

Yes, there are some people who are living awesome lives from their cash flow, but it's not the majority that the "gurus" and magazines want us to believe:

*"All you have to do is find a cash flowing property and repeat."*

Great strategy when it works.

Truth is, most properties don't really have a healthy cash flow until about year 5.

And I mean REALLY cash flow — so that you can quit your job and replace your income.

## The Reality of Cash Flow

I know a lot of people in the real estate industry who are doing extremely well as full time real estate investors. Out of these people, I can probably name only a handful that are actually LIVING off the cash flow of their properties.

That's the reality of cash flow.

It may sound a bit unfavourable now to invest in real estate — but it's important to understand what you're getting into before you spend a large portion of your savings, time, and life trying to become rich from it and "replace your income" like all of the big real estate "gurus" want you to believe.

That said — I'm NOT against real estate clubs or education, at all. Just don't let the "BIG DREAM" of leaving your job in 12 months suck you in.

Believe it or not, MOST of the "full time" real estate investors didn't actually achieve that level of success *because of their real estate*. The fact is, they had an opportunity or were faced with a circumstance that put them in that position.

For me, it was selling my family company, not knowing what to do next, and simply chose real estate as my new career.

I didn't know back in 2005 that becoming a "full time real estate investor" was such a sought-after title. All I wanted to do was learn the RIGHT fundamentals of investing so I could properly build my new business.

If you want to maximize your cash flow, the money you put in needs to be significantly larger.

And most people I know want to put in as little money as possible. Who wouldn't?

Even with the 20-25% I ALWAYS put in as a downpayment, I still find it challenging to find an outstanding cash-flowing property.

But I'm OK with that. Because rather than waiting for the picture-perfect property that delivers massive cash flow, I'm happy to add the average property to my portfolio and let the business take it's course.

All my properties DO cash flow; but throw in a vacancy, or a few repairs, and my cash flow erodes instantly.

*That's the harsh truth.*

The way I combat that is to always put in an extra $4-5K for each property I buy as a buffer (or reserve) so when anything does come up, it doesn't hurt as much. I'm also not pulling money from my joint venture investors or out of my own pocket.

Real estate investing is a BUSINESS, and business income fluctuates. So for me, I'm not "banking" on the cash flow from my real estate at this point in my life to "live."

That's one of the reasons I have a consulting business and sell training programs. I have to keep money coming in from some other source while my real estate portfolio builds. And I suggest you do the same.

# CHAPTER 4

## The Passion Trap

***The Passion Trap*** sounds like a Hollywood movie title to me; but it's not, it's real life.

It's a "life" real estate investors believe they're living — the *"real estate is my passion"* life.

Before we go any further in this book, let's both make sure we're on the same page:

## Real Estate Passion is a Lie

Does that shock you?

*I think most of us are lying to ourselves if we think real estate is our "passion."*

I know this is gonna stir up a lot of emotion and put some people in defense-mode, but <u>that's what I'm after</u>.

Even if you're not in agreement with me right away, it's cool.

I don't expect you to take this book as gospel. There are things you'll be in harmony with and some you won't. I'm not here to promote you dragging your feet, waiting and hoping for something to change in your life.

I feel like I need to stir up some REAL emotion in you.

If you've ever seen me talk live at real estate events, you already know I LOVE to shake things up and get the conversation to a whole new level.

And it's so easy.

All I have to do is say, *"If you think you're PASSIONATE about real estate, think again — you're not. You're EXCITED about it. You're passionate about what it can DO for you, not the actual real estate itself. I'm up for the challenge if anyone thinks I'm wrong."*

The room goes silent...I can see people raising their eyebrows and giving me that glassy stare because I've just offended 80% of the room, if not more.

A few people will always stand up for the challenge, proclaiming, *"No, you're wrong, I am REALLY passionate about real estate."*

## Real Estate is Not YOUR Passion, Either

Let me ask you one question:

*"If you had no more financial limitations, and there was nothing you ever had to worry about, including your health, what would your average perfect day look like?"*

Read that *carefully* before you answer.

Because when I ask the question when I'm speaking somewhere, most people either:

1. Can't answer it, or
2. Get the answer wrong.

**Here's Why**

Number 1 is self-explanatory. They can't answer it because they've never thought about it, or they're consumed with the busyness of just getting by day to day, that they can't even see through the current obstacles in their lives.

But the second one needs a bit of proof, right?

*How would I know* if their answer is wrong?

**Here's How**

When I ask people what their average day would look like if everything were perfect, they usually say something like:

- Travel the world
- Sit on a beach
- Sleep in
- Buy a new house/car/boat/vacation property

That sort of thing...

You know, the stuff we DON'T have right now.

The stuff we WOULD do if we suddenly had some "free time" and won the lottery.

But that's NOT what I asked. I asked, *"What would your **AVERAGE** perfect day look like?"*

The emphasis is on AVERAGE.

In other words, something you would/could do EVERY DAY, and *never get bored.*

I can argue that sitting on a beach every day would eventually become quite boring, right?

The same thing goes for travel, buying a new car, or a vacation property. You're not going to do that EVERY day, are you?

Sure, I understand you may enjoy travelling and you want to see the world, but imagine getting up EVERY DAY, packing, going to another airport, boat dock, or whatever...

Over and over and over.

It's not realistic. It's not an AVERAGE perfect day.

Making sense?

So, most of us answer this question wrongly because we're focused on the EXCITING things we want to do. Sky dive, travel, swim with the dolphins, buy a Ferrari, get a vacation home, and so on.

That's ALL really cool stuff...and whatever makes you happy; but that's more than likely NOT what you would be doing EVERY day, for the REST of your life.

When you CAN answer what your average perfect day looks like, *you've tapped into your passion.*

By challenging people with this inside my private Masterminds and coaching, I've opened up people's minds and hearts to help them discover stuff they've never really been able to see before:

Things like painting, building wells for third-world countries, supporting battered women by building a community shelter, teaching, writing a novel, and so many other inspiring, **real** passions.

That's how I know people are lying to themselves thinking that real estate is their passion.

## Still Don't Believe Real Estate ISN'T Your Passion?

I get it. Because it happens to me all the time when I'm doing this test live with people.

I'll still have someone argue that I'm wrong. *"Real Estate IS my passion!"* they'll proclaim. (By the way, make sure you check out the success story with Monika at the beginning of the book regarding this.)

It just means I have to come at it from a different perspective:

*"How do you KNOW that?"* I'll challenge.

*"I love helping people, and giving them a clean, safe place to live,"* they'll respond.

For the most part, that answer sounds like a marketing tag line they've been fed/practiced at some seminar.

But I'll give them the benefit of the doubt.

So I'll ask them... *"Okay, so if you love helping people, are you going to buy a property with YOUR money, let someone move in RENT FREE, you'll manage it for years, making sure to take care of all the maintenance and repairs — for FREE — and when you finally sell it, IF there's any upside, you'll give away that profit to a charity, or something?"*

*"No F-n way,"* is the standard answer I get back. *"I've gotta make SOME money from it, or else what's the point?"* they'll tell me.

Game. Set. Match.

Real estate is NOT their passion.

Because I highly doubt anyone would get up and go through the motions of searching for a property, buying it, putting tenants in, renovating it, or whatever it is they do if there was NO FINANCIAL GAIN to it.

You with me?

So I GET that real estate investing might be EXCITING for you. In fact, it might be the reason you get out of bed in the morning.

I understand that you get fired up about the deal making, the buying, the flipping, and so on. But I'm guessing you're after the END RESULT...the money — and the FREEDOM the money gives you.

ONCE you have that, you could care less about real estate — I'll bet my last dime on it.

By the way, when I present this way of talk at real estate events, there are always remarkable people who come up to me afterwards to tell me how "real" it was - they'll tell me stuff like *"...I found your presentation very real and honest. You truly have found, and are doing what your purposed to do..."*

And that's what I want for YOU! To do what you're purposed to do!

So it's REALLY okay to say, *"I like the money real estate is going to give me because achieving the freedom to do [x] is my passion."*

*"Achieving the freedom to write my novel."*

*"Achieving the freedom to teach math to kids who are struggling, and their families can't afford a tutor."*

*"Achieving the freedom to take a nursing course so I can help elderly people in retirement homes."*

*"Achieving the freedom so I can fly around the world and speak to thousands of people and help THEM achieve their own success."*

ALL of that without being paid — those sound like passions to me — don't you agree?

Truly dig down and uncover the REASON you believe you're passionate about real estate. What is the REASON real estate is so powerful for you?

What will you GET from building a real estate portfolio?

What will you be able to DO when your portfolio is sufficient to fund your lifestyle?

# CHAPTER 5

## The Sacrifice Trap

(A.K.A. "The I'll Do What Others Won't" Trap)

Have you heard the *"Today I Will Do What Others Won't So Tomorrow I Can Do What Others Can't"* type of quote?

Awesome quote — but real estate investors have bastardized it, simply because they DON'T UNDERSTAND IT.

THEY believe (well, most of the ones I've taught, coached, met, etc.) that it means they need to SACRIFICE their life — or parts of it — to work hard, grind; whatever word you want to use...to succeed.

THAT'S B.S.

Do you know why?

Because I've watched people's "few years" turn into DECADES.

I've seen people's lives fall apart — marriages crumble — relationships with their kids destroyed, or relationships are non-existent because they're "working hard".

The quote actually was meant to **motivate** you and I to DO something — to move out of fear — NOT to spend decades of your life building a real estate business...

That's NOT freedom.

Let me share this with you: there's a HUGE difference between sacrifice and strategy.

"Sacrifice" is described as pain and suffering; it's an **act of giving up something valued for the sake of something else regarded as more important**, such as family and free time.

The average real estate investor believes working later, harder, and spending weeknights and weekends sitting in seminar rooms away from family and friends "for a few years" will eventually give them all the freedom they want.

That is simply NOT the case.

"Sacrificing" for our businesses has a huge personal impact on me.

I grew up watching my father do *everything* he needed to do so he could build his business.

He sacrificed days, nights, weekends, holidays...

I learned a lot watching how hard he worked. He would NEVER give up, even when the company was facing "closing the doors" multiple times.

So I know what commitment is all about.

I also know what *sacrifice* is all about. Because I naturally started living my life the same way; giving up nights, weekends, family functions, vacations, and so on in order to work hard for the freedom I thought I would eventually achieve by doing this.

I didn't realize the difference between *sacrifice* and *strategic commitment*.

It wasn't until cancer "told" my dad at 57 that he had 3 years to "LIVE". *"You better get a life,"* it said.

So not only did I learn about commitment from my dad, but I learned that sacrifice is the *wrong* strategy.

This ONE area is where I will make sure people (you) hear me.

# CHAPTER 6

## How Does A Successful Real Estate Investor Think?

You may be wondering how you can set yourself up for success. The power of a positive mindset takes a bit of work, but it's worth it.

The first step would be to really understand exactly what you want to achieve. Is it a real estate portfolio of 50 doors that brings in $10,000 a month so you don't have to work for someone else? How fast do you want to achieve this? What will it take?

All these questions (and more) begin to define what is most important to you.

You will also begin to define WHAT you need to achieve this outcome. If you have only enough money to buy 5 of those 20 properties, then you now understand the *importance* of putting a plan together to attract joint venture money, because you've attached and aligned the *importance* of JVs to the number of properties you need, and, to the end result you want.

Is this making sense?

Your burning desire to achieve becomes automatic, and you look for solutions based on what you want.

At the same time, you place boundaries around your decisions based on what's important to you.

I find that this is where a lot of real estate entrepreneurs fall off track. They are "sacrificing" the wrong things to get what they THINK they want.

For example, I can't begin to tell you how many people I meet who tell me how stressed they are. They tell me how their life is chaotic trying to balance a job, family, and their real estate investing business — and time is ticking away.

A *success mindset* would begin to put all of those reactionary choices and decisions aside.

I only learned recently how important a positive, focused mindset is. My hope is that this information gets to you earlier than I learned it, so you don't waste half of your life figuring it all out.

In so many instances, I remember sacrificing the "surface level" stuff for "opportunity". I did that because I didn't know where I was headed, or why.

## How Do You Know When You're Successful?

Success is a very **abstract** word, and for most people, it's attached to a **future** outcome.

So how will you know when you're successful?

I've found that most people answer this question with, *"When I..."*

Can you see how a statement that begins with, *"When..."* is attached to the future?

I've noticed that even though highly successful entrepreneurs shoot for specific targets, they DON'T ignore where they are today. Just as importantly, they don't ignore where they were YESTERDAY.

## It's ALL A Test

One of the self-realization exercises I use with my clients is to have them look at yesterday and ask themselves, *"Am I proud of anything I accomplished? Did it move me towards my end result?"*

There's no grey area — it's either "yes" or "no".

An example may be: "Yes, I called a prospective joint venture investor and set up a meeting," or, "I updated all the mortgage balances in my portfolio," or whatever it is...it doesn't even have to be that concrete; it could be something along the lines of "prevention" for your business — making some adjustments to your analysis to react to market conditions in the future, as an example.

The point is to constantly ask yourself: *"Is what I'm doing right now getting me to where I want to be?"*

This helps you realize the importance of the moment; of what is happening NOW...and, helps you realize if you are moving forward or not.

If you constantly live in the future, thinking, *"When this happens, then..."* you are **severed** from the present — and the present is all that is, it's where ALL the learning is happening.

Many people wait for years to pass before they look back to comprehend if what they've been doing has actually built success for them, because ALL their thinking is future-based — they're chasing the next big thing that comes in some thought-based future that doesn't even exist yet.

# CHAPTER 7

## How Do I Get Past The Real Estate Investing Fear?

Real estate investors are commonly afraid of:

- Losing money
- Bankruptcy
- Making mistakes that will impact themselves and/or their family financially
- Alienating friends and family because they've failed

Those are just few off the top of my head, but the fear of *failing* is the underlying theme.

Let me share a quote with you:

*"FAILURE is not the opposite of success, it's PART of success."*

My friend and uber successful entrepreneur Joe Polish says, *"Every time you fail, you are one step closer to succeeding."*

I really want you to understand that *the fear of failing is actually crushing your dreams.* Every moment you stall; you are destroying a piece of your future.

The most successful people I know *welcome* failure and mistakes because they look at it as figuring out what DOESN'T work.

I know it sounds odd to welcome failure, but think about how many times you've tried something that didn't work one way, so you decided to try it another way. If you don't make mistakes, you don't know how to handle things when they come up. So *stepping into fear* is the fastest way to success. Period.

For this to really hit home, I want you to picture a fire-walk scenario — just like the ones Tony Robbins has made so famous. You know what I'm talking about here, right? (Where people walk barefoot over scalding hot coals.)

Why do you think somebody walks over fire? To move out of a comfort zone? To prove they can do it?

To simplify: would you agree that it's because there's *something on the other side* of that fire walk that they want? Whether it's pride, accomplishment, crushing their fear, making good on a promise they made to the other participants...they have an intense emotion driving them to get across those coals.

In other words, they're ALL doing it for a POWERFUL reason.

Let's take it one step further (no pun intended):

Imagine what would happen if someone **stopped** walking while they're in the middle of that fire? It's not difficult to figure out they'd probably burn their feet.

That leads me to believe there's another powerful force at play that's getting them over those hot coals.

Whether they know it or not, their subconscious mind is yelling, *"Get the hell over this fire so you don't burn your ass!"*

Agree?

So this means that motivation has a lot to do with AVOIDING PAIN. It's not JUST about getting the "good" stuff at the end. That's called inspiration. It's great to have inspiration, but I've found more people are motivated when they're moving AWAY from a pain they're already IN than they are when they're attempting to move TOWARD something they haven't yet experienced.

That's why "getting out of the rat race" is a big motivator for real estate investors...because they experience the pain of the 9-5 every day. They want more time off, but they're much angrier that they only have 2 weeks of vacation time a year.

Follow?

That's *emotionally connecting* to the PAIN.

**Your** pain is there. It's always been there. And this is what I'm all about. I'm about helping you pinpoint the pain in your life so you start to MOVE AWAY from it.

And I'm betting that you already know what it is.

Sometimes it's easy to draw out of people, and some need a bit more exploring.

If I've put you in a depressed mood, don't be — let's look at the goal for a moment and why it doesn't really motivate most real estate investors.

When I ask a group of real estate investors what they want, I'll get some form of them wanting to quit their job, make $5,000-$10,000 a month, and live free. Nothing surprising there, right?

So if THAT'S their motivation, why aren't they doing anything about it? One reason is that they allow themselves to have excuses, which really is the *Saboteur* taking over. We'll go over that in a little bit.

What I'm trying to do here is help you connect to the pain in your life. Connect with whatever it is that **you don't want anymore!**

For me, it's about LOSING the freedom that I have right now.

See, I'm very happy with the freedom I have, even though it's not the *best* freedom...yet.

I don't own an island in Fiji, or anything like that, and I *still* want more freedom, but I **don't** want to go BACKWARDS.

That's my pain...having to start again, give up my leisurely mornings, having to wake up and punch the clock, have a boss...that sort of thing.

This also means if I HAD to "live" with what I have right now...I'd be alright with it.

This is the kind of clarity I want for you.

I want you to connect with whatever it is that **you will never, ever do again.**

If we jump back to the fire-walk analogy, what's the scariest part about walking on fire?

If you said the first step, you're bang on. The first step in anything we do is the hardest part, no matter how much Tony Robbins or anybody else encourages you, and gives you the chants, or breathing exercises. When you come face to face with that fire, you're thinkin', *"Jesus I don't wanna to do this, what if I burn myself?"*

Think about it: real estate investing is the same as walking on that fire. You've got all the tools, all the skills, all the motivation, and the support. You just need to take that first step in the direction you're going, and KEEP going!

Because if you don't, what's going to "burn" you? What's that pain you're trying to move AWAY from?

Find that, and you've found your motivation, my friend!

## Finding Your Pain-Motivation

If you're having a bit of trouble finding your pain-motivation, here are a few examples that my coaching clients have expressed over the years:

- Stuck working in a full time job
- Spending the rest of life saying, *"What if...?"*
- I'm not getting any younger — don't want to get old, fat, and feel miserable that life went by
- Restarting life
- Not home enough for my young children
- Want more "me" time — sometimes just be inaccessible to the world for a day or two
- Want to be more active in my kids school (projects, play, social stuff)

WOW, right?

Strong motivation to get moving, don't you think?

## The *Saboteur*

Have you ever wondered how many times a day we give up on ourselves?

Whether you know it or not, we all have limiting beliefs that aid us in the sabotage of our own success, well-being, and happiness.

Isn't that crazy?

WE sabotage our own success.

I don't have the time and space to really dig deep into this here — but I'll give you a brief explanation of how we limit ourselves just with our own thinking.

Recall the section: ***"Committed or Interested"?***

When we're committed to ourselves, NOTHING will stand in our way; but there's a catch...in order to be committed, we need to BELIEVE in ourselves, AND we must be willing accept the good along with the bad. This is where the less successful people struggle.

Our *Saboteur* suggests thoughts and feelings that keep us planted in our lives. It maintains the status quo.

Sometimes it appears as protection, but it's actually preventing us from moving forward and getting what we truly want in life.

Our *Saboteur* will always be with us. It's neither good, nor bad; it just is.

The *Saboteur* loses power over us when we can identify it for what it is, notice our options in the situation, and then consciously choose the action we truly desire at the time.

## Limiting Beliefs

*"Something's going to go wrong, and I can't pay my bills."*

Understanding that we all have the *Saboteur* within us is really important because it's the "little voice" that points out negativity and "warns" us about what could go wrong — which is when it takes on the disguise of the protector.

There are many things that go on inside our minds and our hearts, stopping us from making decisions and stepping into the fear of the unknown.

Sometimes you can really "hear" that voice or "feel" the emotion — and other times it's subconsciously happening, and you don't even know about it.

That's why positive thinking can be so dang difficult. It takes work to get those fearful, negative thoughts out of our head.

**Here's a BIG** *Saboteur* **for real estate investors:**

*"I need to know more about X before I can Y, so I can achieve Z."*

Remember the traps we went over earlier? Well, this is part of it, too.

We let our *inner Saboteur* "keep us safe" by telling us we need to learn MORE.

80% of the people I meet already have enough written down from seminars; yet, they've never gone back to those notes ever again, and they're sitting in another seminar room.

I know it's scary, but you need to go and USE exactly what you already have — all the stuff you've written down and have never gone back to!

Come on, seriously — you have some information, but you don't use it.

Why not?

It's my belief that you're unsure of yourself. Unsure of what might happen. What if you take the step and find out it's not going to work? Isn't that better than sitting on the sidelines wondering if it will work?

Business is not about perfection, getting it right every single time and knowing everything there is to know. You're never gonna know everything, and things are going to go wrong.

It's about testing, making those mistakes, figuring out what DOESN'T work so you never repeat it again. And believe it or not, those mistakes are what BUILDS your confidence, character and more importantly, you real estate business systems and checklists.

In fact, it would scare the shit out of me if an entrepreneur got up and said, *"Listen to me, I'm a millionaire and I've never made a mistake — come invest with me."*

Because when the shit hits the fan, that guy or gal won't know how to adapt.

And that's the problem with a lot of people: they don't know how to adapt because they've never taken the chances, or made the mistakes.

*"What if [X] happens?"*

My answer to that is, *"What if it doesn't happen?"*

Your inner *Saboteur* is powerful — if you LET it take control of your life.

As a matter of fact, every 90 days, I'll give my coaching clients a *"Saboteur* check-in" so they can identify their internal limiting beliefs and take control. Here are some classic ones:

- Disappointed in myself
- Feeling sorry for myself
- Not good enough

All of those (and more) usually come from not achieving a goal within a specific time frame that is usually unrealistic. I remind them how much they've changed, what they've eliminated from their lives, and how far they've progressed.

Be aware of what you're telling yourself daily. If it's negative, it's cool for now — you're normal...just make an effort to swat those negative thoughts away and replace them with positive ones.

Take a moment now and write down ONE limiting belief in your book journal. Start your sentence with, *"My limiting belief is..."*

This will get you ready for the next section.

## Prepare for the Storm

If there's one thing I'm certain of in the business of real estate investing, it's this: **there's ANOTHER storm coming.** The storm is: pressure — fear — anxiety — adversity — and sometimes misfortune.

I'm also certain of another thing: that is, that you and I can weather the storm with a unique mindset, in addition to the fundamentals of sophisticated investing strategies.

Why do so many people say "mindset", and what does it mean? First off, how many people have you come across that discount the entire "positive thinking" culture because their lives just simply get worse?

Stick with me for a few minutes because what I'm going to teach you here are a few techniques I've learned over my several years with top entrepreneurs.

I'm referring to *positive pressure* because we, as entrepreneurs, are going to be faced with a LOT more pressure and stress than most others face in their daily lives. We both know it.

What's important for you to realize, right here, right now, is that the pressure and stress will NEVER stop. You will ALWAYS be faced with some sort of pressure and be hit with misfortune in your business...and in your life.

The MOST important thing is to:

- Accept that it's going to happen, and
- Decide how you'll deal with it.

As a coach helping others build their lives and their business, I have noticed that MOST people run and hide when adversity strikes. Adversity comes in many forms and is dealt with in many ways and described in more ways than one: a dip, a low point, whatever.

However, the most successful people I know have GROWN by stepping into, and accepting the *positive pressure* they're faced with. For me, it started with watching my father — and although it didn't make sense to me when I was 12 years old, it does now.

As I continue to observe all the people I respect and model, they all have that same characteristic: being able to step into and accept positive pressure.

As Bill Phillips says, *"...our character will never be fully tested until things are not going our way. Those who have the courage to succeed in spite of adversity become an inspiration."*

Read those words again — I believe they should be posted on everyone's wall.

Pay attention to the second part of the quote, which is really important. Imagine being the inspiration to others, to your family, your colleagues, customers, and so on.

Once you tap into the inner belief of why you're investing in real estate, you'll discover that you'll be able to overcome all adversity.

I've seen too many entrepreneurs give up on their dreams even though they know full well, DEEP down inside what they should do, but refuse to stick with it because things get too hard.

In other words, they don't live up to the words they tell themselves.

If you do that often enough, Bill also says, *"...your self-trust — your confidence — will fade away."* What happens as a result is we self-doubt, we become anxious, and angry.

# CHAPTER 8

## How Do I Get There From Here?

If you want to get from Point A to Point B, do you agree that sometimes it looks VERY challenging, and sometimes impossible?

What most people do is look at Point B from exactly where they are standing (Point A) and the destination looks too far away. Even though we say we want to get to the dream, when it comes down to actually doing it, MANY people don't have the ability to follow through.

It's because they don't truly BELIEVE they can do it...it's too far fetched, even though they say they believe.

Actions speak louder than words. If you don't have what you want, take a look at what you're doing every day and that will give you a huge insight.

For instance, if you're wanting to quit your day job and replace your income and it will take buying 20 properties to do it, that's a pretty daunting task...right?

Let's break that down for a moment to see what you've got on your plate:

- You need to LEARN how to invest properly
- You need CAPITAL
- How MUCH capital do YOU have?
- You'll probably have to get joint venture investors (JVs)
- HOW do you GET joint venture investors?

As you can see, these are just the basic layers to get you to your goal. When you REALLY truly look at the process, it seems like there's a lot (and we've only scratched the surface).

What I've found working with real estate investors who jump right in and start buying is that they eventually discover: "It's more than they bargained for." Reality begins to set in and many are stopped dead in their journey, overwhelmed by how much they need to do and the length of time they need to do it in.

THAT'S when most of them shut down and start going in circles... maybe that's where you are, too.

I'm here to assure you that you can EASILY get out of this circular chaos.

Let's go back to the Point A and Point B theory again.

When you're sitting at Point A and looking at Point B, you may think, *"I CAN'T see myself there."* I know I've said it multiple times in my life and in my business, and in fact, a few years ago, I NEVER saw myself with a coaching business with clients paying me to help them...but, here I am.

How did I do it?

It's the *framework* we're already starting to reveal.

When you're looking at Point B FROM Point A, thinking, *"I CAN'T get there"* — take a look RIGHT in front of you...look down at your feet — WHAT'S the NEXT immediate step you need to do?

There's ONLY ONE THING between YOU and your dream RIGHT NOW.

What is it? When you identify what that is, you NOW know what needs to be done to move you forward.

Tony Robbins calls this *"chunking"*... taking your HUGE goals and chunking them down to smaller, achievable goals.

What I do with my personal coaching clients is take those smaller achievable goals and break THEM down into weekly tasks and THEN FURTHER into *daily* priorities.

By using this system, let's say you want to buy 20 properties in the next 5 years so you can quit your job. What's the FIRST thing you need to do?

Maybe it's:

- Deciding what TYPE of property you want to buy
- Choosing an AREA to invest that does not add chaos to your life — in other words, you can get to it to look at properties and visit tenants (or your team) when you need to
- Gathering the RIGHT team members to help you delegate the jobs you don't want to do
- If you've already got most of this running, then maybe you need to find capital (joint venture investors)

# Jumping Out of the Comfort Zone: How I Started My Real Estate Business

*"Whatever you do, don't lose our home."*

I was sitting beside my wife just about to sign over $200K to our mutual fund rep at the time, and that's all she said.

I could see the fear in her eyes. But she trusted me.

I didn't know what I was doing. But she trusted me.

I didn't know what I was doing. But I trusted me.

Years earlier, in 2005, I decided to sell my portion of the family company I was VP of.

In 2001, we lost my dad. He was only 60 years old.

3 years earlier, cancer told him, *"You better get a life"* ... because my dad was a true entrepreneur. He sacrificed everything. Every moment. He gave everything he had — including his life. Of course, that wasn't in his "plan".

Throughout my life, dad always wanted me to take over the company. But I had different ambitions. I wanted to be a DJ. And I achieved "celebrity" status; going on to have my own radio mix shows, playing at the top nightclubs, and remixing/producing many of the world's top recording artists at the time — Justin Timberlake, Jennifer Lopez, Whitney Houston, Britney Spears just to name a few...one of my biggest accomplishments was a production with *The Who's* Pete Townsend.

It really was a dream come true.

With all of that happening, I also had a vinyl distribution business with DJ customers all over the globe. I started that business when I was just 19 years old and it went worldwide in 3 years — *without the Internet!*

To say I was *dedicated* is an understatement.

But it also took me away from my son. From my wife.

Even though I was steps away from them in the basement studio, 15 hours a day.

Remember that *sacrifice* I told you about?

I was the king of sacrifice.

I was following in my dad's footsteps. I learned how to be committed to something. To never give up. It's just part of who I am.

But there's a "dark side" to that if you don't understand strategy — it means that all you're doing is fighting to live another day.

In 2003, I decided that music was no longer serving me. Mostly because my second child was born, and the music industry took major hits with the onset of the digital era so it was fairly hard to make a good return remixing artists. Also, the radio station wanted to pay peanuts in order for us to work the crazy hours.

I would hardly ever see my family, and the money I would be making would never support us.

My wife took on the role of the breadwinner more times that I can count. In fact, I could write an entire book about the sacrifices she made, and how hard her days were as she supported me trying to grow the music business throughout the downturn. I love her deeply.

So I crawled back to my mother and told her I needed a job. I told her I was "ready" to take on the family business. Truth is, it was an easy escape into something that would pay me a handsome salary, allow me to have new cars, and provide me with all the perks of owning a corporate business.

But only 18 months later, in January 2005, I had enough of the corporate life.

My life became a living hell. I dreaded going into work every day.

First of all, I lived a 45-minute drive away from work. That doesn't seem like a long time, but for someone who became used to rolling out of bed at 10am every morning and walking downstairs to the recording studio — it was a DRASTIC change.

It became a jail for me. I would constantly be disciplined, I was always questioned about my "style" and work philosophy because people punched in at 8am and left at 5pm.

But I'm not a morning person. In fact, once I got up, I would be working for hours in my home office for hours before realizing *"I need to show up at work."*

I was under a microscope...and I was VP of this company!

I HATED every moment.

My job was actually an obstacle for me to get any work done. In other words, because my family had an impression that I needed to PHYSICALLY be there from 8am to 5pm (for reasons I'll never know), I was never respected for the real work I brought to the table.

In other words, each week's meetings felt like it was an attack on my time card rather than focusing on what value I was truly bringing to the company and how we could grow.

For me, the daily pain was personally associated with family — even though that sounds like a shitty thing to say, it's the truth. For others, they may have some other type of stress at their jobs or careers.

Either way, that stress was there. And I took it home with me every day. I would shout at my wife for no reason. I would be angry with my 6-year-old son. I wouldn't enjoy time with my newborn daughter.

I originally thought that by going back to my family company, I would escape the stress and anxiety of trying to keep my head above water with my music business, and at the same time allow me to expand my father's dream...keeping the legacy of his hard work alive.

But it didn't go that way at all. And I was shell-shocked.

I stepped into something I was unprepared for — something that had too many protocols I was unaware of, and rules I was unwilling to follow.

Because that something was **violating** my inner soul, my true belief in who I really am.

So in January of 2005, I resigned as VP from the company; sold my share of the company, and moved on.

It was the most emotional decision I have ever made...

Like my mentor Brendon Burchard says, *"Only two things change your life: either something new comes into your life, or something new comes out of you."*

Something new was coming out of me. And for the next 3 years, I began my journey into building a legacy for myself, my wife, my children, and their children from everything my father taught me — intentionally and unintentionally.

The best part is, in 2007, we were at a point in our lives that most people fight for every day:

We had a paid off home.

No debt.

A couple of cars.

A few 6-figures in the bank.

What more could we ask for?

How about buying property in the worst economic times we've seen in our lifetime?

## Building A Legacy

I can't ignore that we were in a great position.

But it was about creating a legacy rather than going to Hawaii and spending ten years blowing away all the money, partying and "enjoying life" because "we deserve it."

There's nothing wrong with celebrating your wins, and taking time off and whatever else makes you happy.

But for me, it really was about setting up an ultimate future.

It was summer 2008, and I had just finished 18 months of pure real estate investing education. I had joined an awesome real estate network and met some amazing people who are still in my life today.

Don Campbell, president of REIN (Real Estate Investment Network) at the time, is someone I owe a lot of gratitude. The man and the crew at REIN guided me into investing in real estate the RIGHT way.

I had attended other seminars and workshops where I was told to go to the back of the room if I wanted to receive more training.

I wanted something more for my kids.

And this is what led me to build a real estate business.

I bought my properties in every recent economic "turmoil": 2008-2009, 2011. Not strategically, but just because I was ready.

I started coaching real estate investors in 2011 because I found there was a need to help them build a true business from their real estate — and because I've been an entrepreneur all my life.

Within the past 5 years, I've sat amongst some of the world's top entrepreneurs in Masterminds, and even having some of them as coaches — people like Greg Habstritt, John Assaraf, Eben Pagan, Mike Koenigs, Rich Schefren, and Brendon Burchard to name just a few.

Today, I'm blessed to pay it forward and share this great knowledge and level of thinking to all of my coaching clients.

# CHAPTER 9

## The BIG Picture: What is "Freedom"?

The first things you'll want to do is:

- Know the reason(s) WHY you want to invest in real estate, aside from the money and freedom benefits
- Determine what "freedom" looks like to YOU
- Identify what is important to you TODAY
- Identify the things you're unwilling to give up
- Define how real estate investing is going to FIT into your TODAY lifestyle

If ALL you had was a CLEAR vision of what you're after, you'd be 80% further along than most real estate investors.

Because many real estate investors are clouded by the concept of opportunity, money, and an abstract version of *freedom*.

When Stephen Covey wrote, *"Begin with the end in mind"* — it was one of the most profound and insightful strategies then, as it still is today.

Goals are useful to GET us to the vision, but they're NOT the vision itself.

To say, *"I want more money to have freedom,"* is saying absolutely nothing.

Here's a simple example of a CLEAR vision with stuff thrown in that they're unwilling to give up:

*"I want to build my real estate business to a level of 20 properties that gives me $10,000 a month so I can quit my current job to spend my time with family and friends. I'm willing to build this no more than 10 hours per week, and will not sacrifice my weekends, family occasions, or events to do it. I will not get fat or degrade my health by ignoring exercise and eating fast food because I'm stuck working overtime."*

As you can tell, that's totally opposite to that of people's unclear definition: *"I want more money to have more freedom."*

Having a clear intention of what you want forces you to search for solutions and answers to help you get there.

You eliminate the mindset about chasing what looks like opportunity, and begin using a *concentrated* interest.

Understanding WHAT you want and WHY keeps you moving throughout the tougher days — the days where most others jump ship to try something new.

If you don't have a CLEAR vision of where you're going and why, you are only propelled by goals that are *unfulfilled wants and needs.*

This future-oriented mentality **takes you away from the present moment**, the real opportunities that exist, and the people around you.

## Why Am I Doing This?

The way I see it, when you're looking at starting a real estate business, this is the question you need to really think about before you spend time aimlessly learning stuff.

For a lot of investors — and I'm sure you'll agree — they're investing in real estate for the *freedom.*

Before we dive into WHY you want all that *freedom*, it's beneficial to look a bit further into why you're taking the time to build a real estate investing business.

**Here's an example:**

When I started my real estate investing business, *it wasn't for freedom.* Because I was already used to being an entrepreneur, I spent most of my life without the pain of getting up and going to job I hated.

However, that doesn't mean I don't want MORE freedom!

That's one of the main reasons I'm sharing all my stuff with you here about building a business you don't have to be constantly a part of for it to succeed. I don't know what's true for you — maybe you want to have a MASSIVE real estate company with offices all over the world. Or maybe you just want a handful of properties that gives you enough cash to never have the NEED to go into the office ever again.

My personal "why" is that I wanted something DEEPER with my real estate investing.

I wanted my father's legacy to live on for my kids and their kids. I wanted to build wealth that we could go back to from time to time while we pursued other interests.

And so far, that's what's been happening.

Because real estate is NOT my main thing. That may shock you coming from an author of a real estate book...but just as I've debated elsewhere in this book: **real estate is NOT a passion.**

I know I've said it before, but it's really important you get that.

So what is it for YOU?

WHY are you investing in real estate?

Take the time to jot down your WHYs.

On your first pass at this, I'm guessing it will more than likely begin with surface level things, such as:

- Financial independence
- Better living style
- Quit my job/step away from the 9-5
- Not to worry about monthly bills
- Go on more vacations

But after you get all *that* stuff down, what's left? You've quit your job, paid all your bills, have more time to spend with your kids and family...what are you DOING with that time?

I'll bet if you really think about it, there's MORE that you want from freedom. And *that's* the answer that will benefit you most.

**Let me ask you this:**

Without thinking, analyzing, or giving an answer that you think is "right", what are your TOP 3 values? In other words, what are the 3 things that are MOST important to you RIGHT NOW?

Write down what comes to mind — it shouldn't take you more than 2 minutes.

Because what you can answer in 2 minutes is just as powerful as what you can answer in 2 hours.

**Here's the next question:**

*Are you LIVING your life based on what you've written down?*

I can tell you from most of my experience in training and coaching people...the answer is *"no"*.

You're not a "bad" person because of it — but it's something to be aware of as we go through this book to determine what "freedom" really is for you.

# CHAPTER 10

## How Do I Define MY Freedom?

Even though we all want it, "freedom" is a blurred outcome, because it means something different to everyone.

So we need to establish exactly what YOUR version of *freedom* looks like, if we're going to "break the freedom barrier" together.

If you've attended any reputable real estate investment club, they'll ask you to write out your "perfect" future, envisioning what it would be like after you've purchased all the real estate you need.

To be honest, I have a really hard time with these types of exercises.

Some people have no trouble with imagining how great their life will be in the future. At the same time, a lot of them just STAY inside dreamland.

But I want to come at this a bit differently.

It's awesome to know what your FUTURE freedom looks like, but *I really care about TODAY'S freedom.*

Because **today's** freedom is the ONLY one in which we can live, and, <u>it is what I find real estate investors willing to give up</u>.

That's counter intuitive in my opinion.

*If you want more freedom later, there's no reason to give up your freedom now.*

## Don't Give Up Your CURRENT Lifestyle

In my opinion, there is NO NEED to *give up* your current lifestyle just so you can build a better one in the future.

That's called SACRIFICE. And although I'll be the first to say that you need to **commit** and work harder than anyone else, it does NOT mean you give up your life to do that.

This is where so many people mess up.

To me, building a better future is about expanding what's good and eliminating what's bad about your life *now*.

You don't need to move backwards. You just need to eliminate what's NOT working, what you *don't* like, and MULTIPLY what IS working and what you *do* like.

I've seen my share of sacrifice, personally, and with my clients.

We tend to believe we need to give things up to be successful.

The only things we need to give up are **bad habits** and **distraction**.

You don't become successful in this or any other business by adding MORE. You become successful by REMOVING things, which *does not include* your lifestyle moments.

I'm not talking about the odd late night, or weekend seminar...

I'm talking about the bad habit of late nights, weekends, missing your children's soccer games, skipping family events, neglecting your spouse and friendships...just because you've "got work to do".

So what I want you to do is ask yourself these same 4 questions Brendon Burchard asked of me, that relate to your life RIGHT NOW:

1. What do I need to do LESS of?
2. What do I need to do MORE of?
3. What do I need to STOP doing?
4. What do I need to START doing?

These questions are important to answer because it will build the boundaries in which you are comfortable.

For example:

- I need to do less "studying"
- I need to do more networking
- I need to stop working more than 10 hours a day and on weekends
- I need to start buying

Whatever it is for you, these answers should be affecting your present situation. And it doesn't always have to be about real estate:

- I need to do less reactive stuff
- I need to do more exercising and take multiple breaks every day to slow down the chaos

- I need to stop eating junk food because I'm always "on the go"
- I need to start blocking time for my spouse, kids every day/night where I'm engaged with them... turn off my phone, etc.

This may not be the "real estate strategies" you were thinking of when you purchased this book, but it's TOTALLY an important part of your success, isn't it?

If you're like all of the people I've met and trained, family is right up there as a number 1 priority. So why would you give that up while you're "trying to build" your real estate business?

I'm no saint here. I'm saying this because it comes from experience. Thankfully, I've woken up and am following my own advice.

## The # of Properties to be Free

Like I told you at the beginning of this book, it's not about teaching you "how to do" real estate. But for a moment, I want to address the question about the number of properties to be "free", which is likely on your mind.

For this example, I'm going to use the easy **magic number** of $10K per month because the math is easy.

Let's agree that an *average* property will conservatively give you $100 cash flow at the end of the day.

**That means you have to own 100 properties.**

ONE HUNDRED.

Sure, there's "lots" of people you'll meet who have that.

But take a look at their life.

Is it lavish, or chaotic?

No doubt there are a few who have reached the level of success we all want, and own property all over the world.

However, *this* freedom blueprint is about starting to live NOW without sacrifice at all.

In my opinion, *you don't have to give up everything to start living.*

**Let's break this down:**

- $10,000 a month with $100 cash flow = 100 properties
- $200 cash flow = 50 properties
- $300 cash flow = 33 properties
- $400 cash flow = 25 properties
- $500 cash flow = 20 properties
- $600 cash flow = 17 properties

As you can see, the more cash flow we start to make, the less properties we need.

However, the ratios begin to change dramatically...do you see that?

If you're in the real estate space, having 15 or 20 properties is kind of the "norm" for someone to be considered really successful.

Don't get me wrong, you don't HAVE to have 20, it's just something I want to point out because it's not a big deal for people like you and I to understand that we CAN own 20 properties and more.

The outside world freaks out if we have more than 2.

So taking a look back at that chart, where do YOU feel comfortable?

When I first started in this business, my goal was to own 50 properties...because "Johnny Real Estate" owned 50.

I had NO CLUE how many properties I wanted to own. I just followed the herd.

My point is, if you want to make $10,000 a month, you need to start breaking that down into how many properties (or doors) you need, depending on how much cash flow you're going to have from each one.

Simple, right?

But most people ignore this small exercise and just end up in seminar rooms finding the "best deal".

# CHAPTER 11

## Which Real Estate Investment Niche is Right For Me?

I won't spend a lot of time on the different types of real estate investments because you can do more research outside the scope of this book to help you understand them in better detail.

At the end of this book, I'll give you my personal list of books that I recommend.

But just to give you a list of niches in which you can specialize, here are the most popular:

- Single family homes/townhouses
- Small apartment buildings (up to 50 units)
- Large apartment buildings (over 50 units)
- Multiplex (2-10 units)
- Student rentals
- Condo apartments
- Flips
- REITs (Real Estate Investment Trusts)

With a few Google searches on each of these, you will quickly understand what each one is all about.

And from the information you find, ask yourself:

- How does is affect my current lifestyle
- How does it affect my business expenses? (Contractors, property management, etc.)
- How does it affect the types of tenants I'll get?

Each one will have an affect on your lifestyle and business intention. This is the reason I began this section with the exercise — to figure what's most important to YOU.

## 4 Ways of Making Money in Real Estate

As I've already mentioned, there are tons of books out there that will go into detail about each one of these ways of making money in real estate, and more.

Here are my foundations:

- Cash-flow (rental income)
- Appreciation (property goes up in value)
- Income Tax Benefits (deductions, etc.)
- Mortgage pay-down (reducing the debt)

Each one will have an impact on what you decide to do for your niche.

For instance, when you follow the exercise in the following part, if you decide that appreciation is most important to you, then you might look at flipping a property.

On the other hand, you may look at a great rental area and choose long-term hold properties that will go up over 5 or 10 years, which also gives you a great appreciation.

If it sounds confusing, it is...but just for the moment, because it will all come together for you as you go through the exercises in this book.

What we're doing is shedding more light on how real estate will affect your life so you make the right choices up front.

PLEASE, keep in mind this is only MY personal "coaching" exercise and not the "only" way to look at these "fundamentals" of real estate.

Just humour me for a moment...

## What Real Estate Niche Are You Interested In?

The question always is, *"Which one is the best? Where do I start?"*

The simple answer is: "Whichever is right for you."

I know you can perceive that as a cop-out, but it's the truth.

Because when I began my real estate career, the Rent-To-Own strategy was something that really intrigued me because I could make 3x the cash flow of a standard rental property; and I didn't have to deal with property management, or repairs, or anything like because the tenant would take care of the place because they were going to buy it.

After I tried this approach, I quickly found out there was a LOT more involved than I was willing, or enjoyed doing.

Some of it was:

- Doing the financial work for the tenant approval process
- Meeting tenants to interview
- Finding the right mortgage brokers for the tenant application process
- Finding JV investors to quickly turn the deal around

...And so much more.

I'm not here to teach you about Rent-To-Owns; nor am I an expert at it - although I think it's a great way to make money in real estate. However, it was not for me at that time.

Rather than answering the question of: *"What niche do you want?"* (Such as flips, apartments, duplexes, single-family homes, commercial...)

I would suggest you begin with the end in mind...at least for now.

And what I mean by this is: what do you want your life to look like 12 months from now?

Be realistic.

This is a part of setting a **S.M.A.R.T.** Goal (Specific, Measurable, Attainable, **Realistic**, Time Sensitive).

It's great to have ambition that you'll own a 200-unit apartment building a year from now, and if that's realistic for you, fantastic.

For most of us, it's not.

Even going in and tearing the guts out of a "good deal" property, putting it all back together, and flipping it for a 50-thousand-dollar upside...all while we hold down a full time job...is a bit of a challenge.

So let's get realistic.

Looking at your current lifestyle, your knowledge, what you're willing to commit to, and the expertise you have...what does your life look like 12 months from now?

## The 4 Important Fundamentals of Real Estate According to The Book of Joey

I'm using the word "fundamental" in a different context from traditional real estate investing training.

This section is not to debate which of these are right or wrong, or claim that my perspective about these fundamentals are the only way you should look at it...it's just another way of breaking the pattern of the stuff you may have been subjected to already, and make you *think*.

It's one of the initial challenges I give EVERY real estate coaching client.

So let's get on with it.

For this exercise, I believe there are 4 main fundamentals of real estate:

- Cash Flow
- Tenant Profile
- Location
- Appreciation

Let's both agree right now — they are ALL important!

However, just like I ask each coaching client, I ask you to put them in <u>order of importance</u>.

It's not as easy as it seems, because each one is an essential part of a good real estate investment business.

But let's just have some fun. Put these in the order of importance to you in a notebook.

I'll give you an example of what I mean:

Most people, when looking at that list, would probably jump to "cash flow" as being most important.

I would then ask: *"Are you doing everything you can to get the MOST cash flow?"*

Think about that for a moment.

Because if you say *"yes"* and you're NOT getting the best cash flow...why not?

Investors will tell me *"There's no inventory — I can't find a great deal."*

— Wait a minute.

I know people who can find good deals just by spreading their arms and spinning around.

What do THEY know that you and me don't?

Nothing.

Perhaps their markets and real estate models differ than the most common methods.

For instance, I know a good friend who turns US foreclosures into major profit over and over again. He's been doing it going on 20 years. He buys properties on auction, then rehabs and sells them. And he makes a fantastic living doing it. He rebuilds communities at the same time. It's part of his "passion".

In fact, he's the poster boy for *freedom* in my eyes.

He's happy, has more air miles than anyone I know, and literally lives out of his suitcase because he's flying from one place to another almost weekly.

He has a unique life. And he's one of the exceptions to the "rule" when it comes to real estate and passion.

But I digress — the point is, there's opportunity for cash flow right there.

However, are you READY to do that? Do you want to spend time in parts of the world chasing and bidding at auctions?

Again, there's nothing wrong with it — IF that fits your lifestyle. For my friend, it TOTALLY does.

This is why this exercise is cool — it makes you think on a different level.

## What I Discovered Doing This Exercise

When I do this same experiment, cash flow is the last thing on my list.

I KNOW I can get better cash flow somewhere else. I understand there can be better opportunities out there. But I'm totally cool to ignore them and build a real estate business that aligns with my personality and my life.

I HATE flying. I'm a homebody. I'd rather not travel.

So that means *location* is VERY important to me, and it moves up UP in the list.

Spoiler alert: *location* is my number 1 priority.

It doesn't mean I'll NEVER buy anything outside of my 1-hour radius, it only means I won't do it today.

You might be thinking, *"Joey, why don't you set up teams like you are doing for your current properties?"*

I agree, but there are a few reasons. I want to have the option of driving to my properties within an hour. I want to be able to visit my team and their places of business. And like I said, I'd rather not have to fly in order to do that.

Secondly IF all went to hell and I had to fire my teams, I could *technically* do things myself because the properties are not far away.

I also don't suggest anyone do the management or renovations themselves...but I'm sure you know where I'm going with this: IF my properties are all over the place, HOW would I manage all of them?

That puts a LOT of stress and pressure on someone — and I've seen it more often that I care to admit.

Even though that's an extreme example, just knowing that I could still deal with a major catastrophe (such as losing my property managers) allows me to sleep at night.

Is this getting through?

Please understand, this is MY comfort…it fits MY life.

You don't have to agree.

I'm just pointing it out to you so that you know WHY I've personally chosen location over everything else as my number 1 priority.

This also means I WON'T be looking at deals and opportunities outside my chosen areas.

No matter HOW great they are.

Get me? AND THAT'S REALLY IMPORTANT to understand.

Because I don't waste my time at "opportunity" meetings.

It also means my realtors ONLY send me properties in my 2 areas.

EVEN if there's a great deal just outside of my desired area, they won't send it to me.

Which means I'm not sorting through "deals" every day. I'm enjoying my life.

When a property comes across my desk, it means it FITS my model because it's IN the area I will buy, and it's IN my budget.

Done.

No research needed.

I realize that someone may read this and see this as being "closed minded" to other "opportunities", but I never said that I would NEVER look at opportunities. I am only saying for now that using this framework and automatic system does not make it an opportunity to look at other things — looking at other things is a distraction.

Let's take a look at each fundamental before you decide on your own list.

## Tenant Profile

If you're wondering why I've chosen tenant profile as a fundamental, it's because it will help dictate the TYPE of properties you'll buy.

Because this is another mistake I see real estate investors make: they start with the type of property without analyzing the type of tenants they'll have to deal with. In other words, they might be choosing a property type based on how much cash flow they'll make from it.

Again, nothing wrong with cash flow...I just want to point out my personal perspective on how I'm creating an autopilot real estate investing system.

In my system, I find it's so much easier to decide who YOU want to rent to...and that usually dictates the types of properties to buy.

For example, if you're choosing student rentals because of the awesome cash flow...are you ready to deal with students?

That means your property type will be of a certain caliber.

It also means your area should be specific.

And it means your real estate repairs and maintenance is probably higher than regular, and will be an ongoing process.

There are considerations for every kind of property you can choose.

The point is, if you don't want to deal with students (for this example), then there's no reason to look into student rentals as a niche, is there? There's no reason to waste your time learning about it if you're not interested in renting to them in the first place.

By the way, I want to remind you that this book is not written to debate which real estate niche is better than another (just in case you jumped to this section first). That's YOUR job to decide which one better FITS your lifestyle, expertise, and so on.

I just want to make a point of how important it is to know the type of tenants you want to deal with because each property type will attract different profiles.

Low income property, for example, which you can get "for a deal", will have it's own tenant profile.

Executive townhouses will have another set of tenants that can afford higher rent.

The list goes on, and on.

Personally, this piece is the second most important priority on my list. Here's my reason (again, this is just MY personal opinion and how my real estate model FITS into my life):

I don't want to turn tenants over every year. I want them to stay 5, 10, 15 years.

I want families. Professionals...etc. That means my rents are at the top end of the standard market. They're not executive prices, but they're more than the average place. Why? Because this slight adjustment in rent usually prices out the bargain-seekers and trouble tenants.

It doesn't mean I've never had trouble — it means it's just another filter that I have in place to attract my tenant profile.

I choose areas where my ideal tenants most likely want to rent.

I choose houses they're going to love and treat as their own.

I make sure we (me and my team) respect them and give them the space they need.

We give them birthday cards — gifts at Christmas, and so on.

In other words, these are good, decent people like you and I.

For the most part, we have very little problems with our tenants.

And they stay for a long, long time.

So that's the "set-it and forget it" system we all want, isn't it?

## Cash Flow

Alright, let me attack this one because it's the "master".

First of all, there's NOTHING wrong with having cash flow as your main objective.

I just want you to be sure it IS the most important.

Because if it is, then you should be doing *everything you can* to make the most cash flow possible to achieve whatever it is you're trying to achieve.

But let's take a look at this for a second.

MOST investors I have met want cash flow to replace their income. On average, that means they want somewhere between 5- to 10-thousand dollars a month in cash flow.

I'm not saying it's impossible. But I AM saying it's not EASY as an average real estate investor, buying a property or two every year, to get out of your job in 6 months.

I realize it's not something you want to hear — and of course there will be some people who will disagree with what I'm saying, because they're making good money in their real estate business.

But seriously, I know VERY FEW people like that.

And of the ones I do know, a VERY SMALL percentage have the freedom you and I are talking about.

So if you want to make a lot of cash flow per month, you really have to have a GREAT *system* in place turning over a lot of properties, or have quite a few in your portfolio that are buy and hold properties.

If, like we talked about a bit earlier, the conservative cash flow is $100 per month, even our 5-thousand dollar a month income goal would need 50 properties!!

Not impossible...but it's a BUSINESS.

If you want $10,000 a month, that's 100 properties.

So you need to figure out how you're going to create that $5-10K a month as fast as possible right?

And THAT'S the problem.

Because again, a lot of people are stuck learning everything possible and not doing anything about it.

## Here's How You Find More Cash Flow

I just gave you a typical example of a buy and hold that makes on average $100 per month in cash flow.

You'll need 50 properties to make $5,000 a month.

In that example, how long will it take you to buy 50 properties?

Unless you've got a LOT of money, it's going to take a while.

So the question is, how do you make better cash flow if you don't want to wait years building a buy and hold business?

This is where the clarity comes in. And just like I would ask any coaching client to do, it means buy and hold (in this example) would be removed from your "opportunity" list if you're unwilling to wait.

Let's pretend for a moment you looked at Rent-to-Owns as an alternative. But this time you might make $500 of cash flow per month.

Alright, now you have to buy only 10 properties.

That's better, right? So that would mean you'd start learning more about Rent-To-Owns as a strategy, and forget everything else.

Depending on how that education goes, you should be able to quickly figure out if it FITS into your lifestyle, ability, comfort level, and so on.

Again, I'm NOT suggesting any particular strategy out there is better or worse than another. It's just VERY important to understand all the components around them and how they will AFFECT your life.

What if you don't like the Rent-To-Own model?

Should you get into flipping a property that could possibly make you $5K or more in just ONE flip?

Who knows? Because it can also bomb. In the same way, it can make you 10x that amount.

Are you the type of person that is able and willing to take on that risk? It would mean you have to invest in building the proper teams, trades, and so on to get it all done. (If you want to learn this type of investing strategy, I would highly recommend my friends' Mark Loeffler and Ian Szabo's book: Fix and Flip: The Canadian How-To Guide for Buying, Renovating and Selling Property for Fast Profit )

But what if you're one of the *"Joey, I can do all that stuff myself!"* dudes?

Alright, are you going to quit your job and do it?

*"No, I'll do it at night and on the weekends."*

THINK about that answer. How fast do you think you're going to flip a property when you're working on it during the evenings and weekends?

I'm just being real with you.

If it were me, and I was looking at flipping properties as my main business, I would invest the time and money into a professional course/coach to show me how to do it.

And I'm not talking about the physical part. I'm talking about how to properly set up the *system* and the trades to do it FOR me. I would want to know what to look for so I'm not screwed by anyone.

But most importantly, I'd want to know how to run this business while I'm trying to get out of my job...

Is this making sense?

So the bottom line is, ARE you doing the BEST niche to make the CASH FLOW you say is the number 1 priority?

When things are presented this way to my clients, their tune begins to change a little bit.

## Location

It's been said that the 3 most important secrets of real estate are location, location, location.

It's true.

But location in this context is a bit different. I am referring to how FAR the properties are from you.

Because I've found investors who buy properties in places so far away from them end up with a scattered portfolio of different types of real estate all over the place.

And even if you have other people, property managers, etc. doing the work for you, it's still a LOT of different people to manage.

I find the ones who get themselves into this mess are the ones who are chasing money and "good deals", and totally ignoring how this is going to impact their lives.

And THAT'S the reason *location* is here.

We both know that we need to buy our properties in good locations, so with that off the table, the next thing is how we're going to get to those properties...

For me, personally, this is my number 1 priority: how to GET to those properties.

Even though I know there may be "better" opportunities in other parts of the country that have more cash flow, etc....I prefer to have my own properties within a 1-hour drive of my house.

I don't like to fly...so having them in other parts of the country make no sense to me, even though I would have teams doing the work.

That's because I'm an entrepreneur at heart, and would want to see my properties every few months, personally. The way my portfolio is set up now, I can do that by taking a leisure drive, and it won't cost me the entire day, or even a couple days flying out somewhere.

Can you see how this is important to figure out for yourself?

You don't have to follow MY logic — just your own.

If you don't mind flying or driving to other parts of the country now and then to check up on things — including your teams and their operations — then maybe location is not a high priority for you.

## Appreciation

We ALL want our properties to go up in value, right?

If appreciation is your main objective, are you buying in places that have the best chance of values going up?

Remember, it's NOT just about "buying low" — because you can buy a property on the cheap in lots of places around the country, but is there potential for that property to go up in value?

What are you basing that on? *Gut feeling* is not a strategy.

If you're an investor wanting to get into the "fast money game", banking on appreciation only, it's not as sexy as flip shows on HGTV.

Again, I'm no expert here, but know a LOT of experts in it.

We just addressed this risk factor in the **"Cash Flow"** section. If you're up for that, then all the power to you.

The appreciation I'm talking about here is *long term appreciation* Which means it's a longer waiting game.

If you're getting into real estate to make money on the appreciation, make sure you're setting up the business to sustain itself and grow slowly overtime while you have alternate income.

## Final Thought on Joey's Fundamentals

We've talked a lot about the fundamentals and how I see the importance of truly analyzing each of them to fit into your life.

But it doesn't mean they're permanent.

You could have a cash flow priority for the first 2 years, and then switch to something entirely different.

It's really okay to start your real estate business with one primary goal and then adjust it as you go.

Don't get caught up in the *set it and forget it* mindset right now, because you'll never move ahead that way.

That short little exercise is just to help you become more aware of WHAT you want from real estate at THIS point in your life...AND, how it's going to impact your current lifestyle.

# PART II

# CHAPTER 12

## What Is The Hypersonic Investment Strategy?

Here's the main framework for buying your next property.

It's simple.

There are so many books and suggestions out there on *"how to buy real estate"*, what the "best methods" are, and so on — yet there are more people sitting inside seminar rooms than are out there buying real estate.

Why is that?

I think it has a lot to do with what you've been reading here.

FEAR. OVERWHELM. DISTRACTION.

Fear of failure, fear of the unknown, fear of making a mistake... it goes on, and on. By the way, one of the books you'll find on my recommendation list is *Real Estate: It's NOT for You* by my friend Todor Yordanov. In it, there are real stories from real people about how they achieved their own successes with real estate.

I'm proudly a part of that book (among others) and share in a bit more detail what I'm talking about in Todor's book, right HERE in THIS book.

**Because fear is the number 1 reason people don't buy real estate.**

It's NOT that they don't know how — because they're obviously sitting in seminars and workshops, and, they've bought the books and training manuals.

It's ONLY because they have a fear of making a mistake.

So I created the *Hypersonic Investment Strategy*™ for the sole purpose of pushing people (you) to get out there and do something.

Guess what — YOU ARE GOING TO MAKE MISTAKES. Count on it! If you don't, it means you're NOT progressing.

**IMPORTANT WARNING Before You Keep Reading**

What you're about to learn is NOT a step-by-step process.

Even though in real estate investing, there are many situations in which you need and must follow a step-by-step process, this isn't one of them...which makes this so powerful.

So please don't get hung up on, "What do I do first?"

The following strategy is a framework. This means all the parts work simultaneously. It's something you adapt to your own world, comfort, and capabilities.

The best part is...**you really can't get this wrong!**

# CHAPTER 13

## 1 Investment Niche

Alright — I just prepared you that what I'm about to teach you is NOT a step-by-step process.

However, this first part of the framework is SO important...and, it's where you'll END UP.

So in reality, it's the LAST piece of the puzzle.

Narrowing everything down to just ONE investment strategy (for now) is the ultimate goal of the *Hypersonic Investment Strategy*™.

When I first introduce this to investors, a lot of them get preoccupied with "letting go" of ALL the other "opportunities" out there.

But THAT is the very reason I'm asking you to focus on ONE investment niche to make this strategy work for you.

We both know there's ALWAYS someone doing really well in an investment niche — everywhere you go, you'll meet someone who tells you that what they're doing is the best.

And that **distracts** us.

Let me share a quick story with you to emphasize this point.

When I first started in real estate investing, I listened to everyone tell me how great their niche was.

Student rentals, single-family homes, flipping houses, buy, renovate, hold, refinance...you name it.

I remember looking at Rent-To-Owns as the immaculate, "easy" way to make 5x the amount of cash flow, with very little work to do.

I immersed myself in the subject.

I bought all the books and went to the courses.

A few months later I did my first RTO deal.

Long story short, it all went to hell.

But I learned a LOT in a very short time. Looking at the failure from a *positive* point of view — it would have taken me years to learn the lessons I did in a few short months.

I also learned that it wasn't for me. VERY quickly.

Now I use the Rent-To-Own method as an <u>exit</u> strategy. So it's still within my niche, but it's been adapted to FIT into my real estate investing system.

There's no other reason the RTO strategy didn't work for me, except me.

First of all, I rushed into it. Secondly, it wasn't something I was prepared to do because there was much more entailed than I thought. Specifically math, and 3 types of relationships I needed to build: the mortgage brokers, joint venture investors, and the tenant buyers.

Truth is, I really don't *enjoy* real estate investing.

I don't get *excited* looking for properties.

But that's just me — I'm a **lazy** investor, and I want my investing to be as easy and **hands off** as possible.

More on that later.

Here's why I'm telling you this:

I found an investment niche (in that case it was Rent-To-Own) — dove in, messed up, and found it wasn't for me.

So today, I don't really care WHO tells me how great Rent-To-Own really is, I don't hear them.

Again, let me emphasize: **it's NOT because it's a bad strategy**.

It's because <u>it's NOT for me</u> at this point in my life. It may *never* be, or maybe someday I'll look at it again. But I would have NEVER known this if I didn't concentrate on it to find that out.

Don't sit there and wonder if you should do this or that.

Test it.

## Here's How This Works

Now that I'm comfortable with my investment niche, I buy single-family townhomes in TWO specific areas.

I don't *care* about student rentals. I don't *care* about duplexes, or condos. I don't *care* about flips or anything else except single-family town homes.

Now, if someone picked up this book and flipped directly to this page, they could think I'm "closed minded", when in fact, I'm actually FOCUSED.

Big difference!

Because my model is so simple that everyone in my business knows exactly what to do.

The realtors know what types of properties I want to buy. The property managers know the tenants I prefer. My joint venture money investors know how they're getting their return on their investment... because there's VERY LITTLE fluctuation to what I do.

When someone asks about investing with me, and want to know the numbers, I can EASILY spin it off the top of my head. ¬†Because I BUY the same thing all the time.

Sure, the market grows and dips a bit which will change the ACTUAL (down to the penny) numbers — but for simplicity's sake, people know what they're getting from me — I don't waste time with areas and properties to research.

**Which brings up another HUGE point:**

When a property comes across my desk, I know I'll buy it because my realtor teams have *already done the research!* For lack of a better description, they've been trained to send me stuff I don't have to analyze.

Let me be clear here — it DOES NOT MEAN I don't run it through a spreadsheet, or take a closer look. It's part of YOUR responsibility and due diligence to do that too.

I'm NOT telling you to let go of every piece of your real estate business and let others make these decisions for you. It's your business, after all. Don't bury your head in the sand.

When you can train your teams (realtors, property managers, etc.) to do most of the groundwork for you...that's awesome, right?

So when it comes to my realtors, they won't send me anything that's outside of my areas of expertise, even if it looks like a steal.

Only when I give the go-ahead to expand where and what I'm buying will I ever see something I'm not interested in. That leaves my inbox *FREE of distraction.*

Which brings up another point...

## Pick One and Stick with It

Think about all the hours' people spend in seminar rooms learning about possible investment niches.

Some people are literally there for YEARS...and haven't bought a single property.

That's because they're not sure which investment niche is the "best" one.

They're wondering where the heck to start.

Remember what we covered in **"Which Real Estate Investment Niche Is Right For Me"**. If you haven't done that simple test to help you figure out what's best for you, I would advise you jump back to that section first.

For now, I just want you to PICK an investment strategy and DO it.

FOCUS on ONE for the time being.

I'm not saying do this forever. (I can hear all the, *"Don't put all your eggs in one basket..."* peeps already, LOL.)

I AM saying do it until one of two things happen:

1. You get REALLY good at it. You become an EXPERT, and you build a SYSTEM around it so you can delegate most of it out.
2. You decide it's NOT for you.

Case in point: even though I now invest in TWO separate areas, I didn't START with two. I crushed it in one area, built my teams, systems, and procedures so I could step away and only use 20% of my time to manage it. That meant I could use the other 80% to learn about another area of interest.

I did that ONLY when the first area was capable of sustaining itself.

Do this **one** thing, and I promise 80% of your fear will disappear!

# CHAPTER 14

## 2-4 Investment Groups, Clubs, Memberships, Coaches and Mentors

There's no shortage of real estate groups out there; I know not everyone will agree with me about this, but I'm here to help you MOVE — not paint pretty pictures all day.

Because if you're spending 80% of your time *inside* seminar rooms, networking, learning and so forth...you are NOT DOING ANYTHING PRODUCTIVE.

That might sound what you call "wrong", but believe me, unless you're ACTUALLY doing something like BUYING a property, it's not productive.

This was a totally different perspective for me to learn, too.

Of course, I realize how important networking is, however, like I said, *productivity* comes from actually DOING something with the network contacts that you have.

I've found too many people mix the concept of networking, with *"I'm scared shitless to buy something, so tell me how YOU'RE doing it."*

Listen, you don't *need* to attend **ALL** the meet-up groups. The reason you see the same people in ALL the groups is because they're too afraid to actually get out there and BUY something.

The "learning" and "networking" is an easy excuse to hide behind their fear. That's what it comes down to.

But we don't like to hear the truth — there comes a point where YOU'VE LEARNED ENOUGH!!

When is that point?

If you're following *this* framework, it's between 7-9 months!!! You'll read about this in more detail in a little bit.

KNOWLEDGE is just not enough.

It wasn't until one of *my* coaches pointed out that reading, watching video trainings, and doing home study courses (and so on) is NOT productivity.

I can read all the books I want — and watch months of video training — but if I'm not *doing* anything with it, it doesn't help me one bit, right?

The same goes for you, if you're spending all your time in seminars and workshops.

You have to get out there and DO something with the material you're learning and writing notes about.

THAT'S where the real learning is achieved.

## Two Stages of Learning

Did you know there are actually 2 main phases of learning?

The first phase of learning is when you *cognitively* pick up on something new. It's the, "O*h, NOW I get it...*" phase.

Just like reading this book. You'll more than likely discover something you didn't know before.

But even though you know something you didn't before, you haven't actually learned anything — you've just become *aware* of it.

Learning is not *knowing* something new, nor is it adding any additional content to your brain.

The REAL learning happens when we enter phase 2 and *take* that new knowledge/information and APPLY it to our world. In other words, **you learn from the experience of using the knowledge of which you just became aware**, because it will give you an outcome and effect to analyze on which you make further decisions.

THAT'S the moment you **learn** from your new awareness of something.

## Here's A Real World Example

When you learned how to ride a bike, you probably watched other people do it. Maybe your parents showed you how THEY rode a bike. You *"learned"* the concept that you need to pedal and keep your balance.

But you still couldn't ride a bike, could you?

It wasn't until you physically got ON the bike and **experienced** how fast you needed to pedal so you could keep your balance, that you actually *learned* how to ride a bike.

And so the TRAP a lot of people in the real estate investing world fall into is they think because they've sat through a presentation about buying a rental property with a line of credit, for example, that they've learned how to do it.

They haven't learned how to do it! They just UNDERSTAND the concept, but they haven't learned how it *actually* works until they do it.

This is the area where real estate investors fall off the wagon. They're caught up in the *"What ELSE can I learn?"* If you're asking, *"What else?"* — you're asking the wrong question.

The question should always be, *"How can I test what I now know?"*

## Choosing Your Mentor or Coach

If you're not investing in a coach, you're doing yourself a disservice.

Even a coach has a coach. I spend thousands of dollars per year to have someone else peek into my life and my business — because they'll see things from a different perspective, give me direction and call me on my bullshit excuses for not using what I'm studying.

They help me advance my career 10x over *because* of the perspectives and strategies alone.

This is the framework piece I would caution you about:

You could, theoretically, invest in 3 or 4 coaches/mentors. But what ends up happening is a conflict of perspectives...IF they're all helping you with the same thing.

However, you could have a business coach and a real estate investment coach who shows you how to do a specific niche...like my friend and colleague Pierre Paul Turgeon, who is a Multi-Family Expert at Multi Family Investing Blueprint and can coach you though the entire process!

Let's say you hired him to help you through the multi-family buying process, and you invested in me as your business/life coach (yeah, of COURSE I had to "plug" my own coaching!) — that would be two separate coaches that compliment each other.

Make sense?

The main point, here, is that you don't want too many different opinions. Because opinions are what keep us distracted.

In this process of finding the best coaches and mentors that are right for you, go with your gut. Your bullshit meter is far more accurate than anything else anyone can tell you.

Of course, you want to have someone with a track record and is doing what they SAY they're doing...but it still comes back to how much you gel with someone and the trust you have in them. I recall my very first coaching client Trudi — she hired me because of ME, not my coaching experience — because at that point I didn't have any "true" coaching experience.

## Beware the "Guru" Who Makes It ALL "Easy"

The first seminar I went to had me salivating...I'll admit it.

I was one of the hopefuls who ran to the back of the room to drop my $1500 for a weekend course that would *teach me what they didn't have time for today.*

I didn't feel right about it on the drive home, you know — you just get that feeling in the pit of your stomach.

So I spent the night researching online about the course I just signed up for.

Of course, you have to take *everything* you read online with a grain of salt because you will easily find positive and negative results, as well as reasons for opinions on anything you're researching.

Again, *distraction*, right?

But in my case, the research led me to understand AND believe that I would end up, at the end of the day, paying upwards of 15-20 THOUSAND dollars to learn all the "levels" of real estate, which I wasn't prepared to do.

The company (which is tied to a "reputable" real estate "guru" — geez, there's that word again) based their business on **upsells**...and not *really* in TEACHING real estate investing (that's my personal take on it).

These are people that prey on others, selling the dream of getting rich fast in real estate.

Some even go BEYOND selling high priced courses and seminars, and go straight for the jugular...

...They offer investments in which their students can "get involved".

To no fault of their own, I've literally seen people's lives, savings, and dignity ripped away from them for trusting these crooks.

If you are going to seminars where someone is telling you to "increase your credit limit" or something crazy like that...RUN.

That's just my personal opinion — again.

So I joined a reputable real estate organization here in Canada (which also had a commitment, but nowhere close to 20 grand) and learned everything I needed to learn in about 6 months.

In fact, as I sit and recall this story, I realize I was subconsciously following the *Hypersonic Investment Strategy*™ I'm teaching you now... except that it wasn't created yet!

So when you're choosing your courses and seminars, please be careful about shelling out tens of thousands of dollars to someone who is promising that you'll be rich at the end of the day.

I totally believe everyone should invest REAL money into a coach, but do your homework.

If someone is telling you EXACTLY what you want to hear while telling you it's really simple, but it costs you tens of thousands of dollars, take a closer look.

I pride my own coaching process as being "hard as hell" and "frustrating enough" that you'll want to throw a brick at me every so often (just read the endorsements section for proof) — but without that pain, you're not growing...except it's not the pain of just emptying your pocket without results.

## What Makes A Good Mentor or Coach?

If you ARE going to look at hiring a coach, mentor, or both — it all depends on what you need him/her for.

And, this will come back to your personal *clarity* of what you want in the first place.

WHEN to add them is up to you. There's no right or wrong answer, here.

If I knew what I know now, I would never have waited 40 years to hire MY first coach.

In my opinion, hiring a coach as soon as possible is the best investment you can make.

There are different types of coaches for real estate:

Some will hold your hand and help you navigate through your first few investment properties. They'll show you exactly how they do things, and you can model their systems and borrow some of their teams and resources.

There are other coaches who are there primarily for accountability. A lot of real estate clubs will set you up with some of these coaches, and they're fine — but just be aware they're not really teaching you about the ins and outs of real estate.

There are also real estate business coaches (where I fall into) who will help you build your real estate business properly.

There are also degrees of business coaching, too.

To give you an example, I personally don't teach real estate fundamentals and "how-to". Big surprise, right?

I understand it enough to give someone advice and what my thoughts are...but I'm not the expert in EVERY field of real estate. I leave that to the professionals.

However, what I DO really well is help someone take all of the overwhelm, the choices, and all the chaos, and make more sense of it so they can fit the right pieces into their own lives.

We experience MAJOR breakthroughs in both business and life!

I help them understand the *business* side of real estate; all of the stuff that traditional real estate clubs tend not to teach them in depth so they avoid things like bankruptcy as an example.

And there's no blame there at all. The reason I learned so much from the club I joined was because they focused on what they knew inside and out...FUNDAMENTALS. They taught me what I didn't know about real estate and how to buy it properly.

Once I knew that, I applied my business experience to build my systems and put my real estate business on autopilot so I can enjoy the freedom I have today.

## What 2-4 Really Means

I want to make sure we're both clear on what I mean by *choosing* only 2-4 of something: groups, coaches, memberships, etc.

It does not mean you have a cumulative choice of:

- 2 investment groups/2 coaches, or
- 3 investment groups/1 mentor, or
- 1 membership/2 groups/1 coach

You get where I'm going with this.

If you happen to find 4 awesome meet-up groups that light you on fire, GO to them!

If you want join 3 memberships to help you decide what's best, go for it.

I just want to caution you that the more people involved in the mix, the worse it can end up being.

That's the ONLY reason I've set this guideline as 2-4.

Imagine if you hired 4 coaches or mentors...if they're set out to teach you about the same thing, don't you think there would be some conflict about what they're teaching you?

So this is all about common sense. You'll now know when you're adding too much to the mix by the level of confusion and overwhelm you have.

# CHAPTER 15

## 5-6 Books and Programs

This part is easy. And probably the shortest chapter in the book.

I advise you to read or study 5-6 books and/or programs per year.

That means you would be reading 1 book every 2 months on the subject of real estate.

Or, you would complete a course or home study program every 2 months.

Perhaps it's a combination of the two.

Realistically, there isn't THAT many programs and home study courses out there to keep you busy for years.

Once you understand the fundamentals, and you begin to specialize in your investment model, you'll quickly burn through the material that's out there.

That's totally fine.

This framework I'm teaching you is to get you started and get you moving FAST, right?

The same goes for programs and weekend workshops.

Now that I've just suggested that you limit the clubs and meet-ups you attend, I still believe investing in yourself, and education is an important part of your success.

If you don't invest in yourself, you're cheating yourself out of your freedom.

Are you cheating yourself out of an awesome future because of a couple thousand dollars a year?

Are you not worth $1000 or $2000 a year?

I can't believe it when I hear that from people.

I spent $25,000 to my first coach, and yeah, I freaked out because I could've bought a property with it...well, close to a property.

Think about that, $25,000 to see somebody <u>just four times a year</u>!

But that was *the best move I made* because I truly believe I wouldn't be here writing this book if I didn't invest in myself.

I'm not saying you have to spend $25,000 either — but in my mind, a few thousand a year for specialized programs/coaching, etc. is SO worth it — IF, that is, you're committed and not just interested!

Believe this: **you don't know what you don't know.**

So invest your time reading at least 5-6 books a year.

You can read 1 book every 2 months right? It's not that hard.

I'm reading at LEAST 2 books per month, and I want to make that a standard of 1 book a WEEK.

One of the FIRST programs I invested in was speed-reading from my friend Jim Kwik at Kwik Learning who happens to be the world leader in memory and speed-reading training.

So the time it took me to learn that skill is now producing 10x more of a return because I can absorb content and books 10x faster than before.

And it fits perfectly with the *Hypersonic Investment Strategy*™.

# CHAPTER 16

## 7-9 Months of Research

Here's where I want you to AVOID what I did in the beginning of my real estate investing career.

This is where you can bend the rules a little bit if you're brand new and just getting your feet wet. GO to ALL the clubs, talk to EVERYONE, and network as much as possible.

You NEED to keep an open mind at the beginning.

But DON'T over do it, because you can very easily get lost in all of this.

After a few months (if you're really aggressive), the 2-4 groups you are keen on should be apparent.

Remember, most of the local groups have ALL the same speakers and people...for the most part. So there's really no use in attending every single one of them...unless you're a seminar "junkie" and are hiding behind the "learning" excuse for years!

That said, let's talk about the time you spend in investigation-mode, just for a moment.

I spent 3-5 years ,"studying" real estate.

I was making sure I was going to do it *"right"!*

I'm not saying jump into anything without knowing what you're doing, but there's a fine line between being competent and confident.

Psychologists call this the "Competence-Confident Loop".

When we don't *know* enough about something, we don't feel confident to do anything about it. Our *competence* in it is at a very low level.

So we set out to learn about it — just like in real estate investing. A beginner may not be fully competent about how to analyze a rental property.

Once they are shown how (maybe by getting a spreadsheet to help), they're now confident about analyzing a property.

Follow me so far?

But then what happens is, even though we know MORE than we did before, instead of going out to BUY a property (in this instance), the investor falls into the "Confidence" piece of the loop — which means they're not confident enough to go and purchase a property because they feel as though there's yet ANOTHER piece missing they don't know about. They're not competent about the next piece.

Fair enough when it comes to a beginner investor. I was there. EVERYONE I know was there.

But I'm referring to the investor that is continuously caught in the Confident-Competent Loop.

They are NEVER competent (in their mind) enough to give them the confidence they need to go and DO something!

This cycle is a killer of dreams. It's a time-waster.

It's kinda like the perfectionist syndrome.

Nothing is ever going to be perfect.

But perfectionists (I'm one of 'em) will edit, fix, adjust, learn more, study, and so on to make sure we "get it just right". (By the way, if you find a mistake or typo, so be it — or else this book never would have made the light of day!)

And that just leaves the project, or whatever we're doing, in limbo. It never happens.

Same goes for your real estate investing.

If you've done 7-9 months of heavy research, you've done enough!

I understand that you're afraid — I know you don't want to make a mistake, but let's be real here — you also know when you're avoiding action, or taking what you already know and trying it out.

As I've mentioned, this is not an EXACT science — because if you're brand new...this framework is a bit more flexible than it is for someone who has been sitting in limbo for years.

And YOU know which camp you live in!

If I had the chance to sit with you for 20 minutes, I'd be able to distinguish which one easily — just like I do when I'm facilitating small private Masterminds with real estate investors.

Here's an example of how I helped a Mastermind student reach a bit more clarity about what he wanted to do:

His overall complaint was that he wanted to move faster. Does that ring true for you, too?

I know this a BIG frustration for a lot of real estate investors, so rather than asking him about what he wanted, I reversed it and asked him, *"What is the stuff you don't want to do?"*

Because he was getting caught up in the research phase.

I told him, *"For now, I don't care what you **want**, I want to know what you've found out that you don't want to."*

You would be amazed at how much he had to say. And this is a "newbie."

You see, we always underestimate how much we really know... because he listed stuff on the whiteboard like:

- I don't want student rentals
- I don't want multi-family
- I don't want apartments
- I don't want to buy in the US

The list went on and on, and that's a huge thing.

This is an IMPORTANT lesson: if you want to figure out what you want to do in your life, clear out the stuff you **don't want** first, and that will leave whatever is worth pursuing for you!

One last thing to mention: I agree there are important fundamentals you need to know. And realistically, you can go to ONE weekend event that teaches everything you need to know to get yourself started.

ONE weekend! 48 hours — and you'll know more than most of the population does about real estate investing.

But what happens is that people get stuck in more seminars learning, studying, and wondering what it is they're missing.

I'll tell you what they're missing:

## Speed of Implementation

All it takes to get moving in the real estate investing business is to *trust in yourself* and taking *immediate* action on what you've learned already.

I'll bet if you've been looking at real estate for more than a few months, you've got a notebook or two of notes you've taken.

Have you USED any of it? Did you CALL the people you said you were going to call?

Or are you stuck in a seminar every week writing down new stuff?

In my experience, the latter is true for most people. So you're not alone if that's you. And I'm no angel here, either. I have a lot of notes I never went back to until I learned about the *Speed of Implementation* from Eben Pagan — another one of my mentors and coaches.

It's VERY simple — take what you learn, and IMPLEMENT it within 24 hours.

That DOES NOT mean if you learn about flipping a house that you go and flip a house in 24 hours. (Would be nice though right?) Instead, it means to take SOMETHING from that (or any other) training, and implement it.

To help you with this process, I've created the following sections with questions to ask yourself whenever you're revisiting any of your notes.

## How Do I Implement/Use What I've Learned?

I think this is probably the MOST important question of all.

*"How do I USE what I've learned?"*

Because NOT using the stuff they've learned is the EXACT problem most real estate investors face.

It's the very reason they're sitting in seminar rooms, week after week, night after night, looking and searching for MORE information.

It's because they don't know how to USE what they've learned, or they're too afraid to use what they've learned.

****Shameless Plug****

This is the VERY reason I began coaching real estate investors. I didn't want to teach them **about** real estate, I wanted to show them HOW to use whatever they've already learned.

The reason is because I'm not the expert in ALL the fields of real estate. And I'm not a real estate education coach. I'm a BUSINESS coach that happens to know a lot about real estate. And that means all I have to do is look at someone's real estate business and show them how to make it more productive by clearing away all the distraction and clutter so they know what to focus on first and what to look for next.

It's that simple.

And that's what you have to do. Go back to your notes and your training manuals — and read them. Look for the clues on how you should be using that information TODAY.

Speed of Implementation is one of the simplest golden nuggets I've learned. Less successful entrepreneurs who sit and wait for MORE knowledge wait forever, while successful entrepreneurs put knowledge and ideas into practice IMMEDIATELY.

A LOT of the notes won't apply to you right at this point in time. That's okay. You're looking for something you can do *immediately*. It could be a phone call, getting paperwork ready for a mortgage broker, doing some physical research by visiting an area of interest to invest in...

...Whatever it is, it's there — look for it and go USE it.

Which leads me to...


## What if I Don't Use This Information?

One of the most powerful ways to become more productive and successful is to cut things OUT of your life — not ADD more things.

The same goes for all the information you have sitting in notebooks.

You've probably taken a lot of notes (or you will begin to if you're brand new), and by following the previous question, *"How do I implement this?"* — it may freak you out.

Because sometimes you CAN'T implement it. Or you don't KNOW how to implement it. Again, this is totally cool!

Because all you need to do is ask yourself, *"What if I DON'T do this today?"*

What will happen if you let that piece of information sit?

How will it affect your progress?

But what about the flipside to this question: What happens if you DON'T use the information that you SHOULD be implementing?

In other words, when you asked yourself the question, *"What if I DON'T do this today?"* — and you don't like the answer, it's a huge red flag that it's your next piece to the puzzle.

I find that this was one of the many common problems for most people. They DON'T use the information they should be using because they're always looking for MORE information.

So, by asking yourself this question over and over again after you review your notes (you DO review your notes don't you?), you'll find yourself motivated to get up and do something more than sit around writing even more notes about real estate investing.

## What if I DO Implement This?

This is basically the same question as the last one, but in reverse. I'm asking this in a different way to present the question with a different perspective.

Let me be a good virtual coach, here, and ask you this:

*"What if you DO implement the information you already have?"*

What will happen?

What are the outcomes?

What if you "don't know"?

THAT'S my point. Yes, there could be BOTH positive and negative results from taking action on something, but you'll never know if you don't do it. Hiding inside seminar rooms and taking notes doesn't make you an expert, and it surely doesn't move you any closer to your freedom.

The point of these questions is to make you aware of how much you already know, and what you're avoiding.

I go through this drill with my high-end coaching clients all the time. Whenever they ask me, *"What do I do next?"* — I ask them, *"What have you done that has or has not worked?"*

If they don't have solid concrete answers, or they're giving me theoretical ideas such as, *"Well, I know about [X] but I don't think it'll work for me,"* I'll dig deeper or call them on their bullshit, getting them to actually TRY it.

The more aware you are of how "doing" or "not doing" something that affects you and your business, the better equipped you are to progress in your real estate business.

## 7-9 Months and You're Good

If you follow this framework and spend time learning about real estate, especially putting in the hours we'll talk about in the next chapter, you'll be more than ready — in my mind — in about 7 months to take some ACTION.

I know how scary that sounds to some people because I see so many of the same people doing nothing for YEARS because they're "still learning".

But not you.

I'm here to break you free of that trap.

Again, I want to hold your hand in reality here — **you're going to make mistakes.**

Just be okay with it.

DON'T wait for years to perfect your system or wait until you know everything about real estate investing before you start, because if you do this, you'll NEVER get there. Like I said before, you can actually learn about a real estate investment niche in a couple weeks if you really put your mind to it.

Apart from more complex stuff like buying major apartment buildings or building skyscrapers, or something like that — this real estate investing thing should not take you that long to figure out.

## 2 Great Research Forums For You

While we're on the topic of research, two of the best forums out there, in my opinion, are the Real Estate Investment Network (REIN) forum located at http://www.myreinspace.com/ and Bigger Pockets located at https://www.biggerpockets.com/.

Just so you know, I'm a member of both organizations. No, there's no "affiliate" payment for mentioning them...I just believe they're a great place to start your online research.

I'm sure you can find more, but remember, the answer to overwhelm is NEVER adding MORE.

# CHAPTER 17

## 10 Hours of Research

Here's the last piece of the framework. Remember, there are no steps to this framework aside from using it as a whole to fit into YOUR life.

In reality, you are putting ALL of these pieces together.

For this piece, it's about committing time to your real estate investing business.

TEN hours per week. That's just two hours a day, leaving your weekend free.

So what do I mean by investing 10 hours per week?

An example would be to spend this time:

- Researching on the Internet about an investment area you heard about in a workshop
- Meeting people who may want to invest with you to see what they're after and to help you

get used to "pitching" someone on your real estate deal

- Reading — completing a home study program and reading books, like we covered previously
- Doing odd, but important things like gathering your financial records to have them ready for a mortgage broker when you're ready to buy

There are a number of things you can be doing with your 10 hour a week investment.

However, the one rule is this: spending time in workshops and seminars does not count!

I know we can debate that networking is to find investors, or that learning about a particular real estate investing niche should be considered work; but in my experience, those networking "opportunities" are just excuses to avoid doing the actual work to build the business.

So I'm not saying don't go to workshops and seminars, because they ARE important. I'm just saying those are extra hours you choose to invest outside of committing to working on your real estate business with these 10 hours.

Make sense?

# CHAPTER 18

## How Do I Make This Work For Me?

You've just learned the easiest framework to get you moving towards your freedom.

It may not be the most complex, creative, ground-breaking thing you've ever seen, but it's not meant to be — remember — simple first. Expand and get funky later!

However, I know through experience that most real estate investors are linear people — they want the steps and the playbook written beforehand.

It's great to have the checklists ready in your real estate business, and they ARE available for you — depending on which niche you choose.  But there isn't really a checklist to choose the right niche...

...Outside of what I've taught you in this book.

Because it's so personal.

I gave you 2 main pieces of the puzzle to help you move ahead:

**Choosing the Right Real Estate Niche**, and the *Hypersonic Investment Strategy*™.

Like I mentioned before, this entire book was written with the intention of AVOIDING telling you *"what to do"*. Because when it comes down to it, YOU KNOW.

And if you think I'm out to lunch here, humour me and follow the framework pieces, such as, go to the 2-4 workshops on a consistent basis — sitting inside seminars, reading online forums and books, and investing in a few special training programs — you'll KNOW what resonates and what doesn't.

Trust me.

REMOVE the *"I want to be rich"* idea from your head for now.

Sure, I'd LOVE to say I own a hundred apartment buildings making a ga-jillian dollars a month in cash flow. If you GAVE it to me — if it *landed* in my lap. But we both know that's not gonna happen. I have to go WORK for it and build my own business around it.

It all starts with ONE investment niche right now, mastering it, and expanding your business around it!

## The Bottom Line

If after reading the above framework you're still thinking, *"Yeah, but..."* STOP right there.

Here's how I stop the "Yeah, but..." cycle with my coaching clients...

...I'll ask them:

*What do you want?*

*Why don't you have it?*

The reality is, building your real estate business to a success level that satisfies you and compliments your lifestyle is a challenging venture. It's definitely not as easy as some people want you to believe. If you meet someone who tells you it's a breeze, **take a closer look at their lives.**

From the majority of real estate investors I've met, sadly many of them are still living in mediocrity by trading more time for dollars. Or, they're just constantly running in super speed on the hamster wheel. Either way, they're not getting anywhere fast.

But it really doesn't have to be that way.

The constant "rah-rah-you-can-do-it" motivation speeches are not a big part of what I do because I think that's how a lot of people get into trouble.

It doesn't mean I'm totally negative — far from it. Because I do believe if you follow in the footsteps of others, you can achieve success, and I'll be the first one cheering you on.

But that depends on what YOUR success looks like — right? We've already gone over this.

Up until about 10 years ago, my "success" was based on the hours I worked and the amount of money I made. It was NOT measured by the quality of my life. Not good. And that's another hint.

I confused "activity" and "busy" with success — just like my coaching client Monika and so many others. I was willing to, and DID "sacrifice" *anything.*

Today I shiver when someone tells me they're willing to sacrifice to build their business. In my mind, ,"sacrifice" is NOT the same as *commitment*.

Some people will beg to differ with me, but I know the difference because I've done both. Remember what I said earlier, a "sacrifice" is to give up something of value for the sake of something else (seemingly) more valuable.

The question is: **are you choosing the right value?**

To get where you want to be, it doesn't mean you have give up your life. I would argue your life is pretty valuable, wouldn't you? Yet every week I meet entrepreneurs trading a piece of their life away because they're afraid — not because they don't "know".

Even more unfortunate is real estate investors who chase dreams and outcomes that are not truly their own. They are measuring against an external reference and it makes them the subject to the measurement of others.

Been there, done that — double not good.

# CHAPTER 19

## What Should I Be Most Aware Of?

After understanding all of this, I'm going to share with you what I have found to be the **biggest obstacle** for my clients and students:

Patience.

And if I'm right, it's going to be one of your biggest obstacles, too.

That's because every one of us wants *instant* results.

So if that's not happening now for you, then I highly doubt as a result of reading this it's going to start happening *tomorrow* for you.

I know that's a really pessimistic way of looking at it, but I have to get you grounded. If I don't, you might close this book forever and go searching for another piece of information to read whatever satisfies your comfort zone and promises what you want to hear.

The MOST growth we achieve is when we hear stuff we DON'T want to hear...because it's the stuff we're ignoring.

# Distraction

The second biggest obstacle will be DISTRACTION.

This book has been about teaching you MORE than strategy and steps.

It IS a framework that is going to get you results...but you have to work it. You have to adjust it. You have to make it your own! You have to FOCUS on it.

If you ignore what you've just read and continue to bounce from this to that, you'll more than likely end up like a lot of people you already see, who are sitting beside you in seminars wasting their life away **waiting for the perfect moment and the perfect investment strategy**.

Sorry to be so blunt, but it has to be said.

Even though time and patience is still something you have to deal with, you can overcome the temptation of chasing every opportunity out there.

You can begin to implement this framework over and over again until you've built the real estate empire you want.

Distraction is the single killer of momentum.

It's what actually kills a business.

Because if you're always chasing opportunities or sitting in workshops learning new stuff, you're distracted.

And it's part of the reason you don't move ahead.

As part of my day, which I suggest for everyone, is to do focus sessions of 50- or 80-minute time blocks.

Turn off everything that will distract you. Put on your phone on a timer and just look at doing *one thing*, because there's so much coming at us in the world that we can't focus anymore.

I'm a productive coach myself and I **still** get caught up in distractions.

Although I'm pretty good at recognizing it, I still get caught down rabbit holes now and then. One minute you go to Facebook to research that one thing, and then you're watching cat videos 5 minutes later.

Not good.

There are too many choices, decisions, and opportunities. And that equals overwhelm and fear, and stops you in your tracks. Everywhere you go, you'll be faced with decisions, opportunities, and choices.

Especially when you go to real estate meet-ups and groups. Even if you're focused on single-family homes in Barrie, you'll meet someone who tells you they're kicking ass buying multi-family homes in Texas.

Boom. You're distracted.

You'll think, , *"Yeah, maybe I should go learn about multi-family."*

Please hear me — I'm not telling you NOT to buy different kinds of real estate.

But I **am** telling you for the present, don't buy multi-family properties (in this example) or anything else until you do the ONE thing really well, and build it out.

After that, you can move on to the next thing.

Remember: 80/20.

Spend your 80% right now on learning just ONE thing.

## Just In Case Learning

Remember what I said about distraction? To not get caught up in stuff that *might* interest you?

One of the "secret" formulas I use in coaching someone to help them figure out what's "right" for them is to reverse the process, and ask them to list what they DON'T WANT.

When you consider the things you don't want, **it's so much easier to find what you DO want!**

When I first heard about *"Just in Case Learning"*, I was with Rich Schefren, and I totally related the concept to sitting in seminar rooms, learning about multi-family properties, condos, flips, duplexes, triplexes, student rentals, and whatever else is out there...

JUST IN CASE we're gonna do it later.

What a waste of time.

Don't you agree?

Look, if you're following what I'm suggesting here, you're probably building out a real estate investing system doing something in particular.

I'll use my investment niche as an example.

I invest in single-family townhomes.

Not condominium townhomes.

FREE hold townhomes.

Already, you can see there's a difference. I'm being VERY specific.

This means I don't need to know about student rentals, multi-family unit investing, or any other types...*even though there are TONS of great ,"opportunities" in my area for those investment models.*

Why?

Because it's just an added distraction while I build out my freedom model.

And isn't that what this is all about?

Again, I'm not saying NEVER.

I'm just saying, *"Not now."*

Which brings us to...

## Just In Time Learning

Just in Time Learning is exactly what it sounds like.

WHEN you need to learn something, you go and learn it.

That not only goes for another investment strategy, but it's also relevant to the strategy you're doing now.

See, this is what holds people back.

It's the fear of not knowing everything.

Get over it.

**You're NEVER going to know everything.**

There's always something new that comes up.

Go with what you know and then you'll know WHAT piece is missing so you can go and learn that.

Here's a real world example:

I invest in a city called Barrie.

When I decided on that city, I immersed myself as much as possible to learn what I needed to so I could buy my first townhouse.

I didn't get caught up in the "need to know more before" syndrome, either.

For about a year, all I did was learn, buy, learn, buy...

I created my personal system.

I found all my team members.

And I crushed it.

No, I'm not the *Donald Trump* of Barrie, but I'm VERY well structured in my system.

THEN, I wanted to move to another city. (See how this "expansion" thing starts to work?)

So now I could concentrate 80% of my time LEARNING (just in time) about the new area, and 20% of my time maintaining the other side of the business.

Follow?

So that means WHEN I was at real estate meetings, information about opportunities in OTHER areas outside of Barrie didn't catch my attention at all — UNTIL I was ready to move into them.

Make sense?

That allowed me to become the expert in my area and not become distracted by every other bell and whistle. I suggest the same for you, too.

# CHAPTER 20

## What Are My Next Steps?

The simple truth is: when you truly commit to change your life, the progression you make — even if it's a slow crawl — still moves you further away from where you USED to be.

The continuous reflection as to where you are today — as opposed to where you were 3, 6, or 12 months ago — is obvious.

By the way, if you're NOT celebrating along the way reflecting on what you have accomplished, I think that is a fundamental mistake. It's one of the most important and powerful exercises I do with my coaching clients.

The results are incredible because most of the time we naturally ignore the good stuff, no matter how small, and worry and focus on the negative and what we haven't yet accomplished.

## Most Never Change

You will also discover when you talk with people you've known for years who are basically doing the "same old stuff, just different day" routine, your conversations become more challenging.

Do they truly believe they'll succeed if they stay the same, changing NOTHING?

How many ways can one complain about the same stuff?

I just say, *"If it's not what you want, don't do it anymore."*

In other words, *"CHANGE what you're doing."*

Are the habits and actions you take every day moving you forward — keeping you stuck — or pushing you backwards?

Success is less about what you know and more about what you think and DO.

## Reflect on Steve Jobs

If the passing of Steve Jobs does nothing more than make you realize you **must** live your passion and not care what the world thinks, then he has made the impact he always intended, and his passion lives on.

It doesn't matter whether you liked or disliked the man, Steve's commitment drove Apple, which in turn *changed* the world as we know it; it changed my life and it changed yours, whether you realize it or not — THAT is a **powerful** outcome from one man's commitment.

Committed people have a lot to say because they've been there, they've done that. They have inspiring stories, sad tales, and unbelievable achievements.

Helping others "see" what they do is part of the commitment, and those who choose to do nothing repel — it's just the way it works.

Next time you are lucky enough to be around someone who has taken a step to better their lives, pay attention to how you feel. Are you interested in hearing the tale, or do you look for a way to excuse yourself?

The answer to that question may reveal your true position on changing your life.

## Simple Method To Conquer Fear and Procrastination

Let's face it: we all fear doing something new. However, when we have a positive, deep connection to what it's all for, *fear then becomes curiosity.*

The most successful people are willing to take a step with the information they know today, and see what happens. They know that *nothing* will EVER be perfect.

They understand sooner or later something along the path will get in their way, or break down. When they discover *that* detail, they either stop doing it or FIX it.

With that in mind, I want to share a simple method to help you get past your procrastination and fear inspired by marketing expert Jay Abraham:

*"Everything is a test."*

If you have the success mindset that "everything's a test", you won't be surprised if something fails or you don't achieve astronomical results.

It goes hand-in-hand with the Speed of Implementation method we learned about to get into action as fast as possible.

These two methodologies may not sound ground-breaking on the surface, but believe me...if you begin to employ them in your real estate investing business, they will change your life.

## The Question I Ask That Changes My Life Every Day

It was 2011, my coaching career was JUST beginning, and I was in my private Mastermind with John (*The Secret*) Assaraf.

On a break, I took him aside and asked him: *"If you could give me ONE piece of PERSONAL advice I could tell my coaching clients, what would it be?"*

Without hesitation, he said, *"Ask them what they're willing to trade their life for."*

Read that again.

### *"What are you willing to trade your life for?"*

I ask myself this question **several times a day**. It's hanging on my wall in front of my desk so I see it all day, every day, and never forget it.

In fact, if you've ever seen me speak, or have attended my Mastermind, coaching, or training events, you've heard me repeat this question. Sometimes you've seen me get emotional as I'm sharing the question...

Because it MEANS so much to me.

To me, "What are you willing to TRADE your life for?" — challenges our procrastination and fear to the very core of our existence.

It means that every day we postpone, stay in a job we hate, choose work that can wait over our personal lives — we are trading THAT moment in time for something that does NOT serve us.

And here's where this gets real...

My interpretation is that **at the end of your life**, will you be able to look back at **each** of those moments in time and say, *"Was it WORTH it? Do I regret wasting that moment of my life?"*

I challenge EVERYONE on this.

Because I didn't like the answer I came up with.

Every moment of my life I ask, *"Is this serving me; is this WORTH me trading my time?"*

And that moves me from procrastination; it gives me the courage to step into fear and make decisions about leaving work the next day so I can live my life easier so I don't feel "guilty".

Most importantly, it gives me the FREEDOM to live my life based on MY terms...which has nothing to do with the quantity of cash in my wallet.

*To your freedom...*

# RECOMMENDED READING

The following books are those I would recommend reading to do further in-depth research about real estate investing.

Because this book is not intended to teach what they do.

Here they are in no particular order:

- Real Estate: It's not for You
- Real Estate Investing in Canada: Creating Wealth with the ACRE System
- 97 Tips for Canadian Real Estate Investors 2.0
- Secrets of the Canadian Real Estate Cycle
- Legal, Tax & Accounting Strategies for the Canadian Investor
- What Every Real Estate Investor Needs to Know About Cash Flow…
- Fix & Flip - The Canadian How-To Guide For Buying, Renovating and Selling Property For Fast Profit
- The Canadian Real Estate Action Plan
- Real Estate Joint Ventures The Canadian Investor's Guide To Raising Money & Getting Things Done
- Real Estate Riches
- Investing in Rent-To-Own Property

- 80 Lessons Learned on the Road from $80,000 to $80,000,00
- The Canadian Landlord's Guide – Expert Advice to Become a Profitable Real Estate Investor
- 81 Financial and Tax Tips for the Canadian Real Estate Investor
- Investing in Condominiums – Strategies, Tips and Expert Advice for the Canadian Real Estate Investor
- The RRSP Secret – Defend and Build Your Wealth with This Powerful Investment Strategy
- The Property Management Toolbox – A How-To Guide for Ontario Real Estate Investors and Landlords
- The Ultimate Wealth Strategy: Your Complete Guide to Buying, Fixing, Refinancing, and Renting Real Estate
- The Millionaire Real Estate Investor

Most of these you'll find on Amazon or your local bookstore.

# MEET THE AUTHOR

Serial entrepreneur, author and speaker, Joey Ragona is a #1 Bestselling author, the CEO "Entrepreneur's Secret Weapon" and Founder of Strategic Business Academy, Engaged Investor and creator of the highly acclaimed "Real Estate Joint Venture Presentation Formula". He also leads the High Performance Achievers Inner Circle, a world-class coaching community/Mastermind that has already simplified the lives and businesses of hundreds of entrepreneurs and small business owners with his national level connections and business skills.

With more than 30 years of experience as an entrepreneur, Joey built his first company at 19, and it went worldwide when he was only 23. Simultaneously, he reached celebrity status as a radio and club DJ as well as music producer for 22 years. Joey is a trusted authority when it comes to "new-world" marketing and implementation. Ragona is an in-demand high performance coach and email/digital marketing consultant with a proven track record behind the success of small business owners and entrepreneurs who want structure, systems, personal freedom, life balance, and aim to grow their business fast without sacrificing their lives.

Joey spares no expense to personal and business development spending his time training exclusively with some of the world's highest achievers including Brendon Burchard, John Assaraf from "The Secret", Eben Pagan, Mike Koenigs, Ryan Deiss, Frank Kern, Joe Polish, Dean Jackson, Jeff Walker, Rich Shefren, Jim Kwik and Harvey Mackay to pay it forward and share their sets of tools, beliefs, system and strategies with his clients.

Joey lives in Toronto, Canada with his wife, son and daughter. He loves Bugs Bunny cartoons, walking in nature and reading.

### To Learn More About Joey

**Facebook:**
http://www.facebook.com/joeyragonafan
**Twitter:**
http://www.twitter.com/joeyragona
**Google+:**
https://plus.google.com/+JoeyRagona
**Instagram:**
https://www.instagram.com/joeyragona.businesscoach/
**LinkedIn:**
http://www.linkedin.com/in/joeyragona
**Blogs:**
http://strategicbusinessacademy.com/blog/
http://engagedinvestor.ca/blog/
**Amazon Author Page:**
http://amazon.com/author/joeyragona
**High Performance Achievers Inner Circle Coaching**
http://strategicbusinessacademy.com/business-coaching/business-coach-invite/

### To Contact Joey

joey@strategicbusinessacademy.com

*Thank you for reading this book. If you enjoyed it, would you please take a moment to leave a review at your favourite retailer?*
*Thank you!*